New Labour's Grassroots

Also by Patrick Seyd

THE RISE AND FALL OF THE LABOUR LEFT

Also by Paul Whiteley

DATA ANALYSIS AND THE SOCIAL SCIENCES
(*with Norman Schofield and David McKay*)

HOW VOTERS CHANGE: The 1987 British Election Campaign in Perspective (*with William Miller, Harold Clarke, Martin Harrop and Lawrence LeDuc*)

THE LABOUR PARTY IN CRISIS

MODELS OF POLITICAL ECONOMY

POLITICAL CONTROL OF THE MACROECONOMY

PRESSURE FOR THE POOR (*with Steve Winyard*)

Also by Patrick Seyd and Paul Whiteley

LABOUR AND CONSERVATIVE PARTY MEMBERS, 1990–92 (*with Jon Parry*)

LABOUR'S GRASS ROOTS: The Politics of Party Membership

TRUE BLUES: The Politics of Conservative Party Membership
(*with Jeremy Richardson*)

WITHDRAWN

New Labour's Grassroots
The Transformation of the Labour Party Membership

Patrick Seyd
*Professor of Politics and
Director of the Institute for the Study
of Political Parties
University of Sheffield*

and

Paul Whiteley
*Professor of Government
University of Essex*

© Patrick Seyd and Paul Whiteley 2002

All rights reserved. No reproduction, copy or transmission of this publication may be made without written permission.

No paragraph of this publication may be reproduced, copied or transmitted save with written permission or in accordance with the provisions of the Copyright, Designs and Patents Act 1988, or under the terms of any licence permitting limited copying issued by the Copyright Licensing Agency, 90 Tottenham Court Road, London W1T 4LP.

Any person who does any unauthorised act in relation to this publication may be liable to criminal prosecution and civil claims for damages.

The authors have asserted their rights to be identified as the authors of this work in accordance with the Copyright, Designs and Patents Act 1988.

First published 2002 by
PALGRAVE MACMILLAN
Houndmills, Basingstoke, Hampshire RG21 6XS and
175 Fifth Avenue, New York, N.Y. 10010
Companies and representatives throughout the world

PALGRAVE MACMILLAN is the global academic imprint of the Palgrave Macmillan division of St. Martin's Press, LLC and of Palgrave Macmillan Ltd. Macmillan® is a registered trademark in the United States, United Kingdom and other countries. Palgrave is a registered trademark in the European Union and other countries.

ISBN 0–333–77778–6

This book is printed on paper suitable for recycling and made from fully managed and sustained forest sources.

A catalogue record for this book is available from the British Library.

Library of Congress Cataloging-in-Publication Data

Seyd, Patrick.
  New Labour's grassroots : the transformation of the Labour Party membership / Patrick Seyd and Paul Whiteley.
     p. cm.
  Includes bibliographical references and index.
  ISBN 0–333–77778–6
   1. Labour Party (Great Britain) 2. Party affiliation–Great Britain.
  3. Great Britain–Politics and government–1979–1997.
  4. Great Britain–Politics and government–1997- I. Whiteley, Paul. II. Title.

JN1129.L32 S4393 202
324.24107–dc21   2001059847

10 9 8 7 6 5 4 3 2 1
11 10 09 08 07 06 05 04 03 02

Printed and bound in Great Britain by
Antony Rowe Ltd, Chippenham, Wiltshire

Contents

List of Figures	ix
List of Tables	xi
Introduction: Party Transformation	xv

1 The Blair Project: Setting the Context — 1

Preparing for government: the Kinnock reforms, 1983–1992	4
Preparing for government: the Smith interregnum, 1992–1994	6
Preparing for government: the Blair reforms, 1994–1997	8
Political objectives and commitments	9
The Labour government, 1997–2001	13
Organizational reforms in the Labour Party	19
Attitudes to the Blair government	26

2 The Grassroots Members: Who Are They? — 31

The recruitment and growth of the membership	31
A demographic profile of party members	34
'Old' and 'new' Labour Party members	40
Labour members and voters in 1997	44

3 The Grassroots: What Do They Believe? — 49

The political attitudes of party members	50
Party strategy	59
Law and order	62
Post-materialism	65
Europe	69
Labour members, activists and voters	73

4 What Do They Do? — 77

The contact dimension of activity	78

The campaigning dimension of activity	82
The representation dimension of activity	83
Donating money and party activity	85
Explaining the decline in activism	89
The general incentives model	89
The evidence for the general incentives theory	93
Changing incentives for activism	105
Conclusions	108

5 Activism and Campaigning in the New Labour Party — 111

Introduction	111
Debates about campaign effects in 1997	114
The evidence on local campaigns in 1997	117
Modelling the effects of campaigning on the vote in 1997	121
Simulating the influence of campaigning on the seats won	133
Discussion and conclusions	135
Appendix: the Simulation Model	136

6 What Do the Members Think of the Party and the Government? — 139

Introduction	139
Members' images of the Labour Party, 1990 to 1999	140
Voters' images of the Labour Party, 1987 to 1997	148
Members' attitudes to the modernization strategy	150
Members' attitudes to their own role in the party organization	156
Members' perceptions of the performance of Labour in office	160
Conclusions	166

7 Conclusions — 167

The key findings and their implications	168
Future models of party organization	170
The decline in Labour's core electoral support in 2001	177

Labour's future	181
Conclusions	184
Appendix	187
Notes	189
Bibliography	193
Index	199

List of Figures

1.1	Labour's share of total vote in Great Britain, 1945 to 2001	2
1.2	Working-class electoral support for Labour, 1964 to 2001	3
1.3	Public expenditure as a share of Gross Domestic Product, 1996–2004	15
1.4	Labour's new policy-making system	21
1.5	Tony Blair's satisfaction rating and Labour voting intentions, 1997 to 2001	26
1.6	Mean scores out of ten for Labour's performance in handling public services, 2001	29
2.1	Individual party membership, 1983–1999	33
5.1	Labour vote and campaigning in the 1997 general election	125
5.2	Change in the Labour vote 1992–1997 and campaigning	128
5.3	Labour spending as percentage of maximum and campaign index	129
5.4	Change in the Labour vote 1992 to 1997 and campaign spending	129
5.5	Change in the Labour vote 1992 to 1997 and Conservative campaign spending	131
5.6	Change in the Labour vote 1992 to 1997 and LibDem campaign spending	132
5.7	Simulations of Labour seats and campaigning	134
6.1	The distribution of attitudes to modernization, 1990 to 1999	153
7.1	Satisfaction with the government's policy performance and voting behaviour for working-class voters in 2001	182

List of Tables

1.1	Labour manifesto promises 1997	11
1.2	Labour's performance in elections in 1999 and 2000	27
1.3	Number of Labour backbench rebellions, 1964–2001	30
2.1	Socio-economic characteristics of the membership, 1990–97	35
2.2	Family connections of members	39
2.3	The demographic characteristics of 'old' and 'new' Labour Party members	41
2.4	Social characteristics of Labour Party members and voters	45
3.1	Members' attitudes on the market economy and public ownership in 1990, 1997 and 1999	52
3.2	Members' attitudes to public ownership by gender, age, class, education, activism and year of recruitment in 1997	54
3.3	Members' attitudes on trade unions in 1990, 1997 and 1999	55
3.4	Members' attitudes on defence in 1990, 1997 and 1999	56
3.5	Members' attitudes on taxation and public expenditure in 1990, 1997 and 1999	58
3.6	Members' attitudes on party strategy in 1990, 1997 and 1999	60
3.7	Members' attitudes on law and order and lifestyle in 1997 and 1999	63
3.8	Members' attitudes on law and order policies by class, 1997	66
3.9	Members' attitudes on post-material issues in 1990, 1997 and 1999	67
3.10	Members' attitudes on Europe in 1990, 1997 and 1999	70
3.11	Members' self-placement on a left/right scale in 1990, 1997 and 1999	72
3.12	A comparison of Labour Party members' and voters' attitudes in 1997	74
4.1	The contact dimension of party activism	79

4.2	Members' attitudes to party meetings	80
4.3	Contacts of members with individuals outside the party	81
4.4	Campaigning in the previous five years by members, 1990 to 1999	82
4.5	Members' perceptions of the effectiveness of campaign activities	83
4.6	The representation dimension of activism	84
4.7	Representation of members on outside bodies	86
4.8	Total amounts donated to the Labour Party by members	87
4.9	Summary measures of activity in the grassroots party	88
4.10	Relationships between collective incentives and members' activism in 1997	94
4.11	The relationship between selective incentives and members' activism in 1997	97
4.12	The relationship between members' perceptions of the costs of participation, group, efficacy and activism in 1997	100
4.13	The relationship between expressive incentives, social norms and activism in 1997	103
4.14	The relationship between political efficacy and activism in 1997	104
4.15	Changing incentives for activism in Labour's grassroots, 1990 to 1999	106
5.1	Members' campaign activities during the 1997 general election	118
5.2	One-off election-related campaigning by Labour Party members in the 1997 general election	119
5.3	Members' campaigning and electoral targeting in 1997	120
5.4	Number of members involved in campaigning activities during the 1997 general election in Houghton and Washington East	122
5.5	One-off election-related campaigning by Labour Party members during the 1997 general election in Houghton and Washington East	123
6.1	Members' images of the Labour Party, 1990 to 1999	142
6.2	Perceptions that the Labour Party looks after the interests of various groups, 1990 to 1999	143

6.3	Members' images of the party leader, 1990 to 1999	144
6.4	Thermometer scores for parties, leaders and members of Parliament, 1990 to 1999	146
6.5	Members' images of Labour Party meetings, 1990 to 1999	147
6.6	Labour voters' images of the Labour Party, 1987–1997	148
6.7	Labour voters' perceptions that the party looks after the interests of various groups, 1987 to 1997	149
6.8	Members' attitudes to modernization of the Labour Party, 1990 to 1999	152
6.9	The social and political characteristics of traditionalists and modernizers	154
6.10	Attitudes of members who had participated in policy forums to their experiences in 1999	157
6.11	Members' preferences for methods of forming Labour Party policies, 1999	158
6.12	Members' attitudes to alternative methods of candidate selection in 1999	159
6.13	Approval of the government's record in 1999	161
6.14	Satisfaction with Tony Blair as Prime Minister in 1999	162
6.15	Members' opinions about the most important problem facing the country in 1999	163
6.16	The government's performance on the most important issue in 1999	164
6.17	Government's performance on a specific issue by levels of activism, 1999	165
7.1	Changes in turnout and the Labour share of the vote in different types of seats captured by Labour in 2001	178
7.2	Predicting the Labour vote share in 2001 from community social characteristics	179
7.3	Changes in the Labour vote share between 1997 and 2001 in seats with a high proportion of unskilled manual workers	180

Introduction: Party Transformation

> *The aims set out in this manifesto are Socialist aims, and we are proud of the word... it is indeed our intention to bring about a fundamental and irreversible shift in the balance of power and wealth in favour of working people and their families...* (Labour Party Manifesto, February 1974: 14–15)

> *We aim to put behind us the bitter political struggles of left and right that have torn our country apart for too many decades. Many of these conflicts have no relevance whatsoever to the modern world – public versus private, bosses versus workers, middle class versus working class...* (Labour Party Manifesto, May 1997: 2)

These two quotations reveal the extent to which the Labour Party has been completely transformed over the past twenty-five years. If we look for historical precedents for such a transformation, the only comparable example is the Conservative Party's adaptation to social democracy after the Second World War. Yet that was essentially a programmatic change rather than a structural transformation so that the party's internal procedures and ethos remained largely unchanged and continued to be predominantly that of a pre-democratic, cadre organization. Today in government the Labour Party has a constitution, programme, policies, personnel, procedures and ethos very different from the time it was in government in the 1970s.

To capture the scale of the changes it is useful to consider some examples:

- The party's political objectives, as now defined in its constitution, are 'by the strength of our common endeavour... to create for each of us the means to realise our true potential and for all of us a community in which power, wealth and opportunity are in the hands of the many not the few' (Labour Party, 1996), whereas previously they were 'to secure for the workers by hand or by brain the full

fruits of their industry and the most equitable distribution thereof that may be possible upon the basis of the common ownership of the means of production, distribution and exchange' (Labour Party, 1993).
- The party's 1997 election manifesto stated: 'we see healthy profits as an essential motor of a dynamic market economy' (Labour Party, 1997), whereas both the 1974 election manifestos stated: 'we shall substantially extend public enterprise' (Labour Party, 1994).
- Party members elected Tony Blair as party leader and thus, ultimately, as Prime Minister whereas the previous Labour Prime Minister, James Callaghan, had been elected solely by Labour MPs.
- The proportion of female Labour MPs elected in 2001 was 23 per cent, whereas in the 1974–79 Parliament it was 4 per cent.
- Since 1997 all Labour MPs have been selected as parliamentary candidates by individual party members whereas Labour MPs elected in 1974 had been selected by local party activists.
- Since 1997 no Labour MP has had direct financial support from a trade union whereas 40 per cent of Labour MPs elected in October 1974 had been sponsored by trade unions.
- Trade unions now cast 50 per cent of the vote at the annual conference, whereas they cast 90 per cent in the 1970s.
- The 32-member National Executive Committee is now no more than the managerial arm of the parliamentary leadership, whereas in the 1970s it played a significant role in intra-party politics.
- Constituency party representatives on the National Executive Committee are now elected by ballot of all individual party members, whereas they had been elected by delegates to the annual party conference; furthermore, since 1997 these local party representatives cannot be MPs, whereas from 1945, with two exceptions, they had always been MPs.
- Party members' opportunities to participate in policy making are directed through the national policy forum and its sub-groups, whereas they used to be directed through the annual party conference.
- In 2000 the number of individual party members was officially recorded as 361 000, whereas in 1980 when, for the first time, membership figures were more accurate than in previous years,[1] 348 000 were recorded.

- Joining the party today as an individual member involves completing an application form for 'New Labour', whereas in 1974 it was for 'The Labour Party'.
- Today it is rare to hear the word 'comrade' used in the party's public deliberations, whereas it remained a common feature of the party's public discourse in the 1970s.

How does one explain these momentous changes? Here we suggest five major reasons.

Perhaps the most compelling reason was the loss of four consecutive general elections from 1979 to 1992. This had a powerful impact on the party as it spent the entire decade of the 1980s, and almost the whole of the 1990s, out of office. Even more to the point, in 1983 the party came very close to losing its place as one of the two major parties in Britain, a position it had first established in 1929. Thus the very existence of the party as a major player in British politics was under threat. The subsequent elections of 1987 and 1992 represented only marginal improvements in the party's vote share of 3 and 4 per cent respectively. So there were constant electoral pressures to modernize from the early 1980s onwards

A second factor relates to underlying changes in society, which produced a situation where various socio-economic trends appeared to be working to Labour's disadvantage. A decline both in the traditional manufacturing industries and in the number of trade unionists, a growth of the middle class and a movement of population away from large urban areas to the suburbs, was interpreted by some (for example, Crewe, 1987, 1991) as the cause of a permanent loss of support for the party. In this view the party was potentially in terminal electoral decline.

A third factor was a growing 'culture of contentment' (Galbraith, 1992) among parts of the population. Essentially the growing affluence of a majority of the voters who exercised economic power in the marketplace and were less reliant on public provision created tax resistance. This was especially true in the case of policies designed to redistribute income and wealth in favour of the poor. This reasoning implied that many voters were no longer willing to pay the taxes to fund the public provision of goods upon which social democracy was based.

A fourth factor is globalization, or an increasingly open international political economy which appeared to restrict a national government's attempts to intervene directly in the domestic economy. The experience of the newly-elected Mitterrand government in France in the early 1980s was a salutary lesson. The socialist government had to abandon Keynesian policies and economic interventionism in France in 1982 in response to the reaction of world financial markets. This provided a clear example of the limitations placed upon traditional socialist goals of public ownership and control by international finance capital.

Finally, the collapse of the Soviet regime at the end of the 1980s undermined any belief in the virtues of centralized economic planning and reinforced the view that such planning was bound to fail, making capitalism triumphant in all advanced industrialized economies.

Any one of these factors would have made the party's task of recovery problematic, but the combination of all five rendered it herculean. The fact, however, that a Labour government is now in office, elected in 1997 with the largest parliamentary majority in its history, and then re-elected in 2001 again with a large majority is testament to the party's resilience and resourcefulness and its powers to adapt. It is also an admonition to those determinists who argued in the 1980s and 1990s that the Labour Party was doomed.

How the party interpreted and responded to regular election defeats and to these domestic and international changes was determined by various political factors, the most important being the attitudes and behaviour of the party leadership, the intra-party power structures and relationships, and the factional alignments. So, Neil Kinnock's response to the dilemmas facing the party differed from John Smith's, and Tony Blair's differed from them both. Party reform was initiated by Kinnock and sustained by Smith, but it is unlikely that New Labour would have been born if Smith had lived.

The use of the term New Labour in the previous sentence obliges us to clarify what we mean by it. Both New Labour and Old Labour are contested terms associated with both inter- and intra-party conflicts. New Labour was first used to re-brand the party by Blair and his fellow party modernizers after he had been elected leader in 1994. Since then it has been used consistently by Blair and his colleagues. So, for example, in the early hours of the morning of 2 May 1997, at the election victory celebrations, Blair stated that 'Labour had been elected as New Labour and will govern as New Labour'. Two years later, immediately after the party's poor electoral performance in the European parliamentary elections in June 1999, Blair made clear that the Labour Party's policies would remain '100% proof' New Labour (Blair, 1999).

There are various problems associated with the use of the terms New and Old Labour. First, parties are complex organizations. They are not unitary actors and the political agendas of the personnel involved in parties will often vary. Furthermore, parties are also spatially distinctive. Differences exist between parties at the centre and the localities, and also among localities. So, for example, parties at local government level differ and are not replicas of their London-based, parliamentary counterparts. Similarly, parties in the newly-created, devolved Scottish Parliament and Welsh and London assemblies are developing policies distinctive from the London-based parliamentary party. And, lastly, parties are not united in their doctrinal commitments. As we revealed in our earlier research on Labour Party members (Seyd and Whiteley, 1992), although they structured their opinions around a core set of beliefs they also displayed significant differences of opinion.

The second difficulty with these categories is that those who distinguish New from Old are suggesting something consistent and uniform before Blair became party leader. But as Ross McKibbin (1997) points out

> The history of the Labour Party has been one of almost constant ideological and political adaptation. In this sense there are many 'Old Labours'. The Old Labour Party which Mr Blair inherited, which we might call the Kinnock-Smith Party, was one variety, and it differed from Tony Benn's variety as it did from the Wilson-Callaghan variety. That party in turn differed significantly from Attlee's, which differed even more from Ramsay MacDonald's. And so on.

Third, some of the claims made by the party modernizers, when contrasting New with Old, regarding the nature of the Old Labour Party are highly tendentious and partial. For example, Mandelson and Liddle (1996) exaggerate the extent to which Old Labour was committed to state intervention and public ownership and the role played by the trade unions within the party.

Shaw (1996: 217–18) eloquently elaborates the problem in using these two categories; he argues that they are 'in effect stereotypes... simplified and value-loaded images designed to project a particular view of reality and like most stereotypes... (are) misleading, squeezing and distorting complex reality by neatly parcelling up people into crude categories which... (do) little justice to the diversity of views within the Party'. We share his scepticism regarding the accuracy of these terms. Nevertheless, although there are problems associated with their use, we will use them. We will describe the current party policies and internal party structures as New Labour and it is in this sense that we state that New Labour would not have occurred with Smith as party leader. However, a major objective in this book is to assess whether, on the basis of surveys of the party membership at the beginning and end of the 1990s, a distinction between New and Old Labour is meaningful at the party's grassroots.

Since Blair became party leader in 1994 and initiated the New Labour project he and his party have come under very considerable scrutiny. First, many of the leading personnel have either been the subject of biographies (see, inter alia, Rentoul, 1995; Sopel 1995; McSmith, 1996; Brown, 1997; Routledge 1998, 1999; Kampfner, 1999, MacIntyre, 2000; Langdon, 2000) or have themselves published autobiographies (Blunkett, 1995; Robinson, 2000). Second, the party's ideas and policies have been exhaustively scrutinised from various perspectives (Thompson, 1996; Taylor, 1997; Panitch and Leys, 1997; Shaw, 1996; Driver and Martell, 1998; Hay, 1999; King and Wickham-Jones, 1999; Ludlam and Smith, 2001). Third, some of the bitter personal rivalries among ministers at the very top of the Blair government have been minutely examined (Rawnsley, 2000). Finally, the party's electoral strategy has been considered in detail by the principal figure involved (Gould, 1998).

What has been missing from these studies has been any extensive consideration of the impact of the New Labour project upon the party's membership. There has been considerable speculation, with claims and counter-claims regarding numbers, levels of activism and opinions, most of which reflect intra-party positions and tensions, but there has been little hard evidence upon which to base these speculations. We do know that there was a 40 per cent growth in membership between 1994 and 1997, but we know little about why these new members joined and whether they would continue to remain as members over time. Claims have abounded that members have become increasingly disillusioned with the Blair government and they are therefore either failing to renew their membership or are dropping away from party activity. On the other hand, counter-claims have been made regarding New Labour's popularity. Speaking at the party's national policy forum in July 1999, Robin Cook asserted that 'New Labour is more popular and is reaching those parts of Britain with which Labour previously failed to connect' (Cook, 1999).

Our purpose in this book is to examine whether New Labour is reaching down and winning support among its own parts, namely among its own members, and whether the Labour Party is a declining and an increasingly inactive grassroots organization. Our arguments are based upon data obtained from four national surveys of party members, the first conducted in 1989/1990, the second in 1992, the third in 1997 and the fourth in 1999 (see Appendix for the details). With these surveys we can contrast Labour's grassroots at the beginning and end of the 1990s and we can address the question of whether or not New Labour is a meaningful term at the grassroots.

In Chapter 1 we examine Labour's modernization strategy from Kinnock onwards in relation to the party's principles, policies and organizational structures. After analyzing the politics of the Labour Party which led to Blair's New Labour, we trace some of the key policy initiatives after the party's return to office in 1997. These help to provide the context for our later assessment of the current state of the party's grassroots. In subsequent chapters we consider the party membership in detail. In Chapter 2 we present a social and political profile of New Labour, comparing and contrasting the members who joined the party since Blair became leader with the long-standing members. Then, in Chapter 3 we consider the political attitudes of party members and, in particular, whether any significant changes in their attitudes have occurred over time which would confirm the existence of a New and an Old Labour. In Chapter 4 we look at the levels of activism and campaigning of members and we ask whether newly-recruited and long-standing members differ and, in particular, whether new members are much less active than their longstanding colleagues.

After our consideration of party activism, we turn to an examination of election campaigning. Increasingly in general elections from 1987 onwards the Labour Party developed a reputation for its highly-professionalized campaigning activities. Labour's 1997 general election campaign was no exception as it targeted seats and used its members as mobile ground troops. In Chapter 5 we examine Labour's 1997 general election campaign and ask whether the target seats strategy was effective in influencing the vote.

On 2 May 1997 the public euphoria over Labour's election victory was considerable, especially so at the party's grassroots. After four consecutive election defeats and 18 years in opposition, the party was at long last back in government. Previous Labour governments of the 1960s and 1970s very quickly experienced difficulties in office and were forced to modify their policies which left many members disillusioned and demoralized. Did something similar occur when Labour entered government in 1997? In Chapter 6 we examine members' attitudes towards the Blair government.

Finally, in our concluding Chapter 7, we consider some of the recent trends and ask whether the Labour Party is becoming more of an 'electoral-professional' organization (Panebianco, 1988) or more of a 'plebiscitarian' organization. In particular, we assess whether the party is increasingly becoming hollowed out at the grassroots and, if this is the case, does it really matter? Does the party any longer require members and activists or are they characteristics of a twentieth-century, mass party now redundant in the post-modernist, twenty-first century? On the other hand, if grassroots members remain important for a democratic party then what needs to be done to recruit more members?

1
The Blair Project: Setting the Context

As we point out in the Introduction, the Blair project produced huge changes in the Labour Party both in terms of its organizational structure and in relation to its policy concerns. To understand the causes of these changes the Blair project must be set in a context of an examination of Labour's electoral support over time.

The twentieth century has been claimed as 'the Conservative century' (Seldon and Ball, 1994). It is certainly true to say that Labour's electoral record between 1945 and 1997 was pretty dismal in comparison with that of the Conservatives. In the 52-year period between 1945 and 1997 the party won only six of the 14 general elections and was the governing party for just 15 years. Furthermore, as can be seen in Figure 1.1, the overall trend in the party's electoral support after 1970 was decidedly downwards. Surprisingly enough, the landslide victory of 1997 was won with the same share of the vote which the party achieved in 1970, when it lost the general election.

That downward trend highlights the fact that what had been historic strengths during the period when Labour became the established alternative to the Conservatives in the 1920s had increasingly become weaknesses by the 1970s. Thus the party's base of working-class voters had steadily eroded both absolutely and relatively over time. In absolute terms working-class voters declined as a proportion of the total electorate from 51 per cent in 1964 to 35 per cent in 1992 (Heath, Jowell, and Curtice, 1994: 281). In fact the working class had never been uniform in its support for the Labour Party, and the Conservative Party's ability to attract a significant number of such voters had been crucially important in explaining its electoral success; nevertheless

2 The Blair Project: Setting the Context

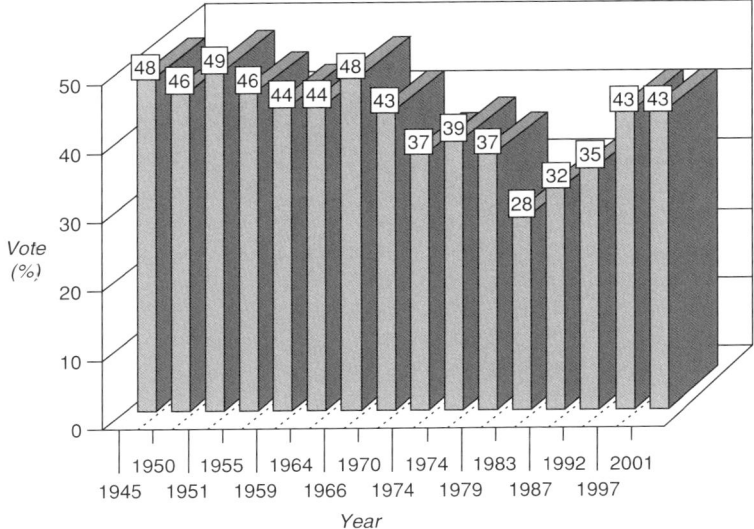

Figure 1.1 Labour's share of total vote in Great Britain, 1945 to 2001

working-class identification with Labour provided the bulk of the party's electoral support. However, from the 1960s onwards the proportion of the working class voting Labour declined, as can be seen in Figure 1.2, and after both the 1983 and 1987 general elections Ivor Crewe (1987: 5) could claim that 'the Labour vote remained largely working class, but the working class was no longer largely Labour'.

A second factor contributing to the downward trend in Labour's electoral support was the formal attachment of many trade unions to the party. This institutional relationship between trade unions and the party had established a sense of community between individual trade unionists and the Labour Party which reinforced their Labour-voting tendencies. This also enabled Labour leaders to argue that there were special ties between the party and the trade unions resulting in tangible benefits for a Labour government which were not available to a Conservative government. So, for example, Harold Wilson claimed in the 1964, 1966, and 1974 election campaigns that his governments would introduce an incomes policy or a social contract, agreed with the trade unions, as a result of this special relationship.

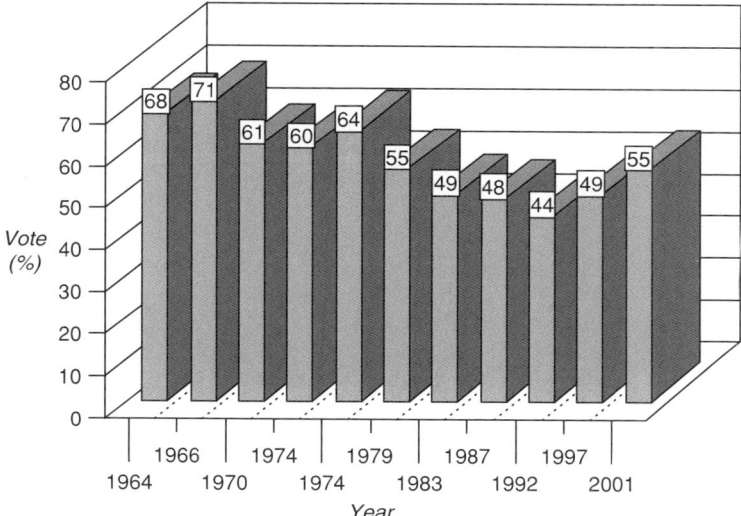

Figure 1.2 Working-class electoral support for Labour, 1964 to 2001

But from the 1970s onwards these formal links were becoming more of an electoral handicap as the absolute number of trade unionists declined and as the trade unions became increasingly unpopular among sections of the population. In addition, increasing union militancy in the 1970s and 1980s was politically embarrassing for the Labour Party. The industrial conflict in 1978–79, commonly referred to as 'the winter of discontent', and the miners' strike in 1984–85, were two instances where the Labour Party suffered from its formal links with the unions.

A third factor contributing to the Labour Party's declining share of the vote was its internal divisions. Labour had always been a factional party as a result of both its ideology and its structure. The struggles of the 1950s and 1960s between fundamentalists and revisionists are a clear example of the intense intra-party divisions which have always been a permanent feature of Labour's history. For a period in the late 1970s and early 1980s, however, the divisions were even more intense than normal and a bitter civil war broke out in which participants felt that the enemy was more likely to be within the party than outside. Comradeship was very noticeably absent and for many voters such a divided party was an unelectable party.

By 1983 the party came very close to being relegated from its dominant two-party position among the British voting public, when it won just 28 per cent of the vote, only two percentage points ahead of the Social Democrat/Liberal Alliance parties. Another heavy election defeat in 1987 prompted some commentators to argue that the party appeared to be doomed (Crewe, 1987: 5). Nevertheless, from the electoral low points of the 1980s the Labour Party steadily recovered its electoral support and by 1997 had again re-established itself as a major player in electoral politics. How it came to achieve this over these 14 years provides the essential backdrop of this book.

In this chapter we will, first, examine the reforms to both the party's policies and structures introduced from 1983 onwards in an attempt to re-establish its electoral support. We will consider reforms as they occurred under the respective party leaderships of Kinnock, Smith and Blair because each leader brought differing perspectives, strategies and objectives to bear on the task. Then, after examining the initiatives preparatory to government, we will look at some of the key features of Labour's governmental programme since 1997 and their impact upon the party's grassroots.

Preparing for government: the Kinnock reforms, 1983–1992

Kinnock was a party reformer who prepared the ground upon which Blair's New Labour project was created. He was compelled to do this after the party's 1983 electoral debacle in which voters, particularly Labour's traditional working-class voters, had defected to the Conservatives in large numbers. They had been attracted by the Conservative's commitments to lower taxes, the sale of council houses and the reforms to the trade unions, and at the same time had been put off by Labour's commitments to nuclear disarmament, to extensive public ownership and to British withdrawal from the European Community (Crewe, 1983).

Kinnock's reform of the party was a two-stage process, in which the speed of reform was limited by intra-party constraints, such as the organizational power of the trade unions and the Labour left, and by Kinnock's own left-wing political past and views. In the first stage, between 1983 and 1987, he modified some of the party's 1983 manifesto commitments. He managed to temper the party's opposition to the European Community, to tone down its promises of public ownership and to abandon its opposition to council house sales, but the party's non-nuclear stance remained. He also initiated moves to expel Trotskyist infiltrators from the party, but was defeated in his attempt to introduce one-member–one-vote (OMOV) procedures for the selection of parliamentary candidates.

Only after the party's 1987 election defeat were major changes introduced. Between 1987 and 1992 a complete policy reappraisal occurred and significant changes occurred in three main areas. First, the party's non-nuclear policy was abandoned. Second, the party shifted away from its historical role of protecting trade unions' collective legal immunities and replaced this with a policy of protecting the rights of individuals at work. Third, the party made clear its commitment to the market economy, with state intervention promised only where market forces were not working. These major changes led one academic commentator to describe the policy-review document, *Meet The Challenge, Make The Change* (1989) as 'the least socialist policy statement ever to be published by the party' (Crewe, 1990).[1]

At the same time as initiating these policy changes Kinnock also maintained a momentum on internal party reform. While continuing with his campaign to expel Trotskyists from the party, he also initiated the process which led to the abandonment of the party's historic commitment to collective, delegate democracy by introducing ballots of individual members to select parliamentary candidates and to elect the party leadership. In addition he extended the leadership's powers to intervene in the selection procedures for the party's parliamentary candidates.

None of these reforms to the party's policies and structures were introduced without opposition from within the party, but Kinnock was assisted in his objectives by the fragmentation of the Labour left and by the support of many senior trade union leaders desperate to see the end of Conservative governments. Furthermore, as we will see later in this book, it is also clear that the party's individual members were weary of permanent opposition and were willing to adapt their views on some issues in order to win electoral support.

By 1992 Peter Mandelson, at that time the party's Director of Communications, felt able to claim:

> We have now effectively completed the building of the new model party... The product is better, the unity is real, our democracy is healthier, our grassroots more representative and the whole outlook now geared to the realities of government rather than the illusions of opposition. (*Guardian*, 16 February 1990)

Nevertheless, Labour still lost the 1992 general election. The party's failure to win this election was a serious blow to its morale because the Conservative government had presided over an economic recession, and intra-party divisions among Conservatives had been rife since the removal of Margaret Thatcher as party leader. Explanations of the remarkable Conservative victory vary, but the Conservative Party's replacement of Thatcher with John Major in 1990, voter uncertainty about Labour's competence to govern, and Kinnock's relative electoral unpopularity were all significant factors (Heath, Jowell and Curtice, 1994).

While, therefore, Labour's proximity to electoral annihilation in the 1983 general election is crucial in explaining the party's subsequent adaptations and reforms, its failure to remove the Conservatives from office in 1992 even after such changes is of critical importance in explaining the emergence of New Labour. This failure reinforced the belief of a small group of party modernizers, who subsequently succeeded to positions of leadership, that nothing less than the complete abandonment of the old social democratic norms – interventionist government, redistribution, working-class support – was necessary. However, the two years under Smith's leadership was an interregnum period before the modernizers succeeded to positions of leadership and went on to introduce fundamental changes.

Preparing for government: the Smith interregnum, 1992–1994

After Labour's 1992 general election defeat and Kinnock's subsequent resignation, the momentum for party reform under Smith's leadership slowed. Among the new party leadership the 'one last heave' school of thought prevailed. This strategy implied that the correct policies and structures were essentially in place and therefore all that was required was effective political presentation.

There has been some speculation as to whether Labour would have won the 1997 general election had John Smith remained the leader and not died so tragically in 1994. In the Gallup Poll of May 1994, shortly before Smith had his fatal heart attack, Labour led the Conservatives in the voting intentions series by 48 per cent to 24 per cent (Gallup, 1994: 3). In addition, while 74 per cent of the electorate were dissatisfied with Major's performance as Prime Minister (19 per cent were satisfied), only 31 per cent were dissatisfied with Smith's performance as leader of the Labour Party (49 per cent were satisfied) (Gallup, 1994: 3). Finally, 49 per cent of the voters at that time thought that Labour would win the next general election, compared with only 31 per cent who thought that the Conservatives would win (Gallup, 1994: 7). These figures suggest, although they do not prove, that Smith's leadership would have produced a Labour victory in 1997, although perhaps with a smaller majority than Blair obtained.

The one significant reform introduced during the period when Smith was leader was the abolition of the participation of affiliated trade union members in the choice of parliamentary candidates in 1993. New party rules were also approved obliging both trade unions and constituency parties to ballot both their political levy payers and their members in leadership elections and then to divide the votes accordingly between these groups. This new procedure would be used for the first time to elect Blair and John Prescott as leader and deputy leader in July 1994. Individual members were also given the powers directly to elect constituency and women representatives to the party's National Executive Committee (hereafter NEC).

Labour's popularity during the period of Smith's leadership was in part due to the Conservative government's ejection from the European exchange rate mechanism in September 1992. By October 1992 Labour's lead over the Conservatives was 10 per cent and this grew over time during Smith's leadership. Such a lead in the opinion polls reinforced Smith's belief that his party had adapted sufficiently to restore public confidence in its ability to govern. If Smith had remained as leader Clause IV of the party constitution would not have been amended, nor would the party have promised to maintain the Conservative government's public expenditure programme for the first two years of a Labour government. It is also very unlikely that the party would have given a commitment to freeze the level of personal income tax in the lifetime of a parliament. On the other hand there would not have been a dramatic growth in the party membership after 1994. Overall, it is fairly clear that Smith's Labour Party was not New Labour.[2]

Preparing for government: the Blair reforms, 1994–1997

A small group of party modernizers, the most prominent being Tony Blair, Gordon Brown, Peter Mandelson, and Philip Gould, did not share Smith's sanguine views. They believed that the party was unelectable while it still maintained some of its policy commitments and structures. For them the Labour Party retained a 'dogmatic, activist-driven culture' (Mandelson and Liddle, 1996: 55) and remained too committed to a centralized state, to public ownership of industry, to high personal taxation and public expenditure, to representing the trade unions and the working class, and to equality of outcome and rights without responsibilities (Mandelson and Liddle, 1996: 17–28).

In their view fundamental change was necessary if the voters were ever to elect a Labour government. Gould made this very clear in a memorandum, entitled 'The Unfinished Revolution', written soon after Blair became leader (Gould, 1998: 238–45). None of this was apparent, however, at the time of Blair's campaign for the party leadership following Smith's death. The personal manifesto that Blair issued as the basis of his leadership bid emphasized the need for a dynamic market economy, full employment, fair taxation, investment in education and training, quality public services and reform of state institutions but it did not signal further reforms. However, he concluded his appeal to members by stating that:

> Labour must exist not only to defend the gains of the past, but to forge a new future for itself and our country. Our job is to honour the past but not to live in it. I have never believed that Labour's essential principles and values were its problem. On the contrary they still retain their validity and their support amongst the public. But the public have longed for us to give modern expression to those values, to distinguish clearly between the principles themselves and the application of them. That is the difference between honouring the past and living in it. (Blair, 1994)

After becoming party leader and initiating major changes within the party, Blair consistently maintained that his task had been to reinterpret his party's principles in modern times rather than to reject them altogether.

We do not intend in this chapter to provide a complete coverage of Labour's policy commitments before and after its general election victory in 1997. Rather, we will concentrate upon a limited number of policy issues which we believe capture the essential features of New Labour and demonstrate the seismic shifts that occurred within the party. We will examine the changes to the party's political objectives as contained in its constitution, as well as some of the party's most important commitments in taxation and public expenditure, welfare, law and order, and education policies prior to the 1997 general election. We will then examine how these commitments were translated into government policies. In addition, since the people most closely associated with New Labour also argued for reform of the party organization, we will also consider changes to the party's internal structures both before and after the 1997 general election.

Political objectives and commitments

Blair's decision to rewrite Clause IV of the party constitution, or more specifically that part which committed the party to 'the common ownership of the means of production, distribution and exchange', was initiated at the party's 1994 annual conference. Although the clause was of no relevance to Labour's policies in government and had little electoral saliency, its symbolic importance as a socialist touchstone within the party was considerable, as Hugh Gaitskell had discovered to his cost when he had tried to rewrite it in 1960 (Bale, 1996). Kinnock would have liked to remove this clause but preferred to let sleeping dogs lie. Blair eventually succeeded, after considerable opposition from his party activists, in replacing the original four-line clause with a 37-line one. Gone was the specific commitment to public ownership and in its place was a commitment 'to create for each of us the means to realise our true potential'. However, as with the previous clause, the new one's importance was more for its symbolism than anything else and, in this case, its demonstration to both political opponents and party activists alike that the party would have no difficulties in managing an efficient and successful market economy.[3]

More important from the point of view of policy outcomes was the decision taken by Blair and Brown, four months before the 1997 election, that a Labour government would neither increase rates of personal income tax in the lifetime of a parliament nor alter the Conservative government's planned public expenditure commitments during its first two years in office. In addition, Labour's election manifesto also made clear the party's resistance to any notion of increasing public spending as the means of resolving economic and social problems by stating that 'the level of public spending is no longer the best measure of the effectiveness of government action in the public interest' (Labour Party, 1997a: 11). With these commitments Blair and Brown hoped to dispel voters' fears that Labour remained a 'tax and spend' party.

New Labour's shift away from the traditional social democratic commitment to increase public expenditure was also apparent in its welfare policies. As can be seen in Table 1.1, which highlights some of the party's manifesto commitments, rather than improve cash benefits for particular deserving groups in society, it stressed its commitment to welfare reform and its aim to provide greater work opportunities, particularly for the young and lone parents, with the aim of reducing welfare dependency (Labour Party, 1997a: 19). The party's objective was not to be too identified with welfare recipients but rather more with taxpayers.

Similarly, the party wanted to be seen to be tougher in dealing with criminals than had been previously been the case. As shadow Home Secretary between 1992 and 1994 Blair had coined the phrase 'tough on crime and tough on the causes of crime' and this became the guiding principle of the party's penal policies. The party emphasized more its concern with the victims of crime rather than the causes of crime, such as poverty, unemployment and homelessness, and it proposed to penalize criminals by adopting tough sentencing policies.

Once Blair became party leader a significant shift occurred in the party's policies on schools. In the past Labour's traditional response to the problems of varying educational attainment had been to propose structural solutions, such as the abolition of the eleven-plus examination and the introduction of comprehensive schools. Now,

Table 1.1 Labour manifesto promises 1997

The economy
'We see healthy profits as an essential motor of a dynamic market economy...'
– no rise in basic or top rates of income tax
– cut VAT on fuel to 5 per cent
– no VAT on food, childrens' clothes, books, newspapers and public transport
– maintenance for two years of the previous Conservative government's public expenditure commitments
– a levy on the excess profits of the privatized utilities
– introduce individual savings accounts
– reform the Bank of England
– establish Regional Development Assemblies
– establish a minimum wage
– workforce ballots to establish trade union recognition

Welfare and health
'The best way to tackle poverty is to help people into jobs...'
'We want to save and modernise the NHS.'
– job training for all under 25-year-olds unemployed for more than six months
– basic state pension to rise in line with prices
– tax rebates for employers who hire long-term unemployed
– raise spending on the NHS in real terms every year
– end the internal market in health care
– end waiting lists for cancer surgery
– ban tobacco advertising

Crime, law and order
'We will be tough on crime and tough on the causes of crime'
– halve the time taken from arrest to sentencing for young offenders
– introduce parental responsibility orders for young children
– stricter punishment for serious repeat offenders
– introduce a new offence of racial harassment
– appoint an anti-drugs supremo
– legislate, with free vote, to ban handguns

Education
'Standards, more than structures, are the key to success'
– increase the percentage of national income spent on education
– nursery school places for all 4-year-olds
– reduce class sizes for 5, 6 and 7-year-olds to 30 or under
– close failing schools
– create educational action zones
– right to study for all under 18-year-olds in work
– introduce student maintenance fees

however, educational standards became the party's main concern and both Blair and his education spokesman, David Blunkett, stressed the need to maintain high standards in all schools and to facilitate parental choice of schools. The party wanted to be identified more with parents making choices in the best interests of their children. In this context, both Blair's and Harriet Harman's highly-publicized decisions not to send their children to local state schools reinforced this message.

Philip Gould, the party's principal adviser on public opinion and attitudes after Blair became leader, makes it very clear that New Labour was targeting two distinct set of voters. First, the 'aspirational classes', or more particularly, the 'aspirational working class in manual occupations' and, second, the 'middle class' and, again more particularly, 'the increasingly insecure white-collar workers with middle-to-low level incomes' (Gould, 1998: 122, 174 and 396). He believed that these were the people who had sustained the Conservatives in office for 18 years. In addition, Blair went out of his way to gain the support of the media, in particular from the Murdoch mass newspapers, and thus to neutralize some of the intense hostility of key sections of the print media towards the party in recent elections.

We have already referred to Kinnock's and Smith's attempts to minimize the power of party activists. Under these two leaders reforms had been introduced to reduce the meeting-attender, activists' powers to select the leader of the party, parliamentary candidates and members of the NEC. After Blair's election as party leader, balloting of members was extended beyond the selection of personnel to policies as well. Blair appealed directly over the heads of activists on his proposal to rewrite Clause IV of the party's constitution and he then used it again to endorse the party's 1997 general election manifesto.

In addition, Blair gave greater priority than his two immediate predecessors to the recruitment of individual party members. Both Kinnock and Smith had talked of recruiting new members, but few party resources had been directed towards the exercise. Blair provided both more commitment and more resources to the task because, firstly, new members would help counter Conservative claims that Old Labour was still lurking in the background, secondly they would reinforce the number of electoral foot soldiers required to target the constituencies necessary to win the general election and, thirdly, his own constituency party in Sedgefield had already demonstrated that a proactive membership-recruitment strategy could attract large numbers of new members (Smyth, 1996).

The Labour government, 1997–2001

> The class war is over... (T)he 21st century will not be about the battle between capitalism and socialism but between the forces of progress and the forces of conservatism. (Blair, addressing the Labour Party annual conference in 1999)

Any idea that Blair and his modernizing colleagues might have been playing down their socialist commitments merely to win an election were very soon dispelled. In government the party leadership remained committed to its pre-election positions on the economy, welfare, law and order, and education. Its policies on these matters were principled and not merely tactical.

It is not our intention in this book to examine in detail the policies of the Labour government during its first term of office; rather, our purpose is to assess the extent to which New Labour's roots are firmly grounded within the party. So we intend to concentrate more upon the key debates and points of discussion within the party during the time after Labour was elected into government in 1997. For this reason we propose to consider only the same limited number of policies as in the previous section, namely the economy, welfare, crime, and education. We will also examine the major structural changes made within the party since 1997. Our main objective is to provide a framework within which we can then assess whether the membership shares the leadership's goals.

The economy

> You cannot build the new Jerusalem on a mountain of debt... (J)ust as you cannot spend your way out of recession, you cannot, in a global economy, simply spend your way through a recovery either. (Gordon Brown, addressing the Labour party annual conference in 1997)

> Stability, long-term prudence, and a dynamic supply side are key building blocks for prosperity... (Gordon Brown, Mansion House speech, June 1998)

Gordon Brown, as Chancellor of the Exchequer, and the most powerful member of the government after the Prime Minister, had three distinctive economic objectives. The first was to establish a fiscal and monetary stability in order to reassure international markets. The second was to create a more competitive economy by stimulating the supply side of the economy and improving productivity. And the third was to stimulate employment.

An important, initial initiative upon becoming Chancellor was to pass responsibility for managing interest rates and for achieving an inflation target set by the government over to the Bank of England. Brown's hope was that by creating an independent Bank of England he would reassure investors that sound economic strategies would not be compromised by political interference.

During his first three years as Chancellor, Brown appeared to revel in the title of the 'iron chancellor' as he declared his task to be keeping public finances under control, balancing the current budget, bringing public debt down towards 40 per cent of GDP, and making low inflation his key objective. His desire to avoid what he frequently described as previous governments' records of boom and bust meant that, with the exception of boosts to educational and health spending in 1999, he refused to sanction any significant increases in public expenditure until 2000. Only then did he propose that planned public expenditure between 2000–01 and 2003–04 should increase by £43 bn. However, as can be seen in Figure 1.3, Brown reduced public expenditure as a percentage of GDP during his period as Chancellor and at the time of writing overall public expenditure is not planned to return to its pre-1997 share of GDP until 2003–04.

In addition to freezing levels of public expenditure in the first years of the government, Brown also maintained the party's pre-election commitment to not raise the level of personal, direct income tax. By April 2000 he felt able to lower income tax by introducing a new starting rate of 10 per cent on the first £1500 of personal income and by also reducing the basic rate to 22 per cent. However, notwithstanding these lower rates of personal tax, in 2000 the Treasury publicly acknowledged that the overall level of taxes had increased since Labour came to office. Tax levels had risen by stealth as indirect taxes, in particular value added tax, excise duties and national insurance contributions, had been modified.

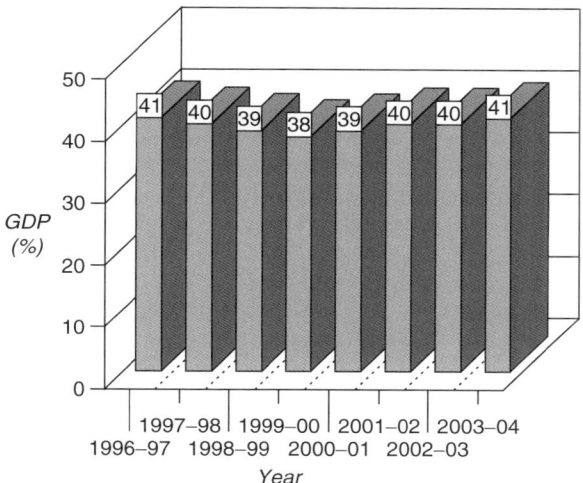

Figure 1.3 Public expenditure as a share of Gross Domestic Product, 1996–2004

In order to encourage enterprise among companies and individuals, the government cut company taxes, initiated employee-shareholding incentive schemes, and created the University for Industry (UfI) as one means of developing a more skilled labour force. Government measures to generate employment included the removal of unnecessary tax and benefit barriers to work and the promotion of skills training. However, the government's welfare to work programme was the priority in this area because people in work would be less likely to suffer from poverty and a dependency culture.

In December 1999, Blair claimed that 700 000 more jobs existed than in May 1997 and over the same period long-term unemployment had been halved (*Guardian*, 30 December 1999) and Brown claimed that 'A return to full employment was once a dream... (but) it is now not only a promise but a possibility' (Brown, 1999). By March 2001 the unemployment rate had fallen below one million, for the first time since 1974.

Brown's major successes as Chancellor were to preside over and manage an economy which grew at an annual average rate of 2.6 per cent between 1997 and 2001, and to establish Labour's credibility with financial markets. When previous Labour governments in the 1960s and 1970s had announced public expenditure increases, they had been immediately faced with instability in the financial markets and a drop in the trading value of the pound as institutional investors displayed their hostility to the governments' measures. No such responses occurred either in July 2000 or April 2001 when he announced increases in public expenditure. His critics, however, claimed that the public expenditure increases should have come earlier and then, when they did come, they should have been larger.

Welfare reform

> I believe in greater equality. If the next Labour government has not raised the living standards of the poorest by the end of its time in office it will have failed. (Blair, 1996)

The centrepiece of the Labour government's welfare programme was the 'New Deal' scheme. The party had promised that 250 000 young unemployed would be found jobs in the first term of government by using £2.5 bn from the tax levied on the 'windfall' profits of the privatized utilities. By 2001 the government claimed that 288 000 young unemployed had been found jobs on this programme (Labour Party, 2001). Critics, however, argued that the degree of compulsion was too great; for example, unemployment benefit is lost if the young person does not attend the continuous counselling and training. Another criticism was that jobs would be created anyway in a growing economy without this particular initiative, and the cost of providing each job was too high.

In addition, the government introduced new welfare benefits schemes, the most prominent of which was the working families tax credit scheme which involved combining taxes and personal allowances in such a way as to benefit families in households with low-income earners. In addition, the government introduced a new childcare allowance, raised child benefit, created a new minimum income guarantee for pensioners and introduced a statutory minimum wage of £3.60 per hour in April 1999.

While, on the one hand, the government introduced schemes such as those mentioned above to target particular deserving groups, on the other hand, it attacked what it regarded as the 'something for nothing' culture. A part of the government's Welfare Reform Bill, approved in November 1999, proposed that benefits to single parents and to the disabled should taper off very rapidly once the recipients obtained other, relatively low, forms of income such as a private pension. This would ensure that the benefits would only go to those in the greatest need. These proposals led to major parliamentary revolts among Labour backbenchers (see later in this chapter). The government's critics argued that the measures merely redistributed resources among the very needy rather from rich to poor, which would be achieved by taxing the better off and using such money to increase overall levels of public expenditure.

One other issue on which the government faced constant criticism from within the party was its refusal to link old-age pensions to the level of earnings rather than to the level of prices. The link between earnings and pensions had originally been broken by the Conservatives in 1981 and since earnings had consistently risen faster than prices over this period, a link to average earnings would provide significantly more income for old people. But the government was opposed to any general increase in pensions, preferring to target those they regarded as in most need. As we will see later in this chapter, the opportunities for critics of the party leadership to mount an effective opposition within the party at either the NEC or the annual conference had been severely restricted. Nevertheless, at the party conference in 2000 the leadership suffered a rare defeat over its pensions policy.

Welfare provision was an area in which the government faced very strong criticisms from within its own ranks. Many expected that the neglect of the unemployed, the sick, the disabled, single-parent households and the elderly during previous Conservative administrations would now be reversed. Ministerial responses to demands from within the party to alleviate the difficulties faced by such groups stressed the need for reform of the welfare system. The argument was that half a century after a Labour government had introduced a comprehensive welfare system based, in part, upon the principle of universal provision, such a commitment was now no longer possible. But the sacking of two ministers in the health portfolio – Harriet Harman and Frank Field – reflected the dilemmas and difficulties the government faced as it tried to balance the demands of universal provision with the increasing demands for better services.

Education

>...we aren't in favour of putting this issue (selection of children at the age of 11) over standards. The total commitment and energy of the government will go behind raising standards in all schools (David Blunkett, *Guardian*, 13 March 2000).

As the quotation from David Blunkett above demonstrates, the government's main objective was to raise educational standards in schools. This was to be done by introducing an extensive system of testing pupil performance, by comprehensive school inspections conducted by OFSTED, and by rewarding good teachers and eliminating bad teachers. By 2001 pupils' standards had improved, as measured by reading and numeracy skills at the age of 11, and GCSE passes at the age of 16. Furthermore, additional teachers employed in primary schools meant that class sizes had been reduced.

Critics argued that the government's policies were failing to tackle social inequalities which underlie poor pupil performance and were therefore placing too much emphasis on what could be achieved in the classroom. In particular, the party's traditional view that comprehensive schooling was an essential guarantee of educational opportunity had been abandoned in favour of encouraging parental choice.

Blair's hostility to comprehensive schools was apparent when he claimed that 'Too often...(they) adopted a one-size-fits-all mentality – no setting, uniform provision for all, hostile to the notion of specialisation and centres of excellence within areas of the curriculum' (*Guardian*, 9 September 2000). Critics complained that the commitment made by Blunkett prior to the 1997 election to end selection of pupils at the age of 11 had been abandoned, and that the procedures which allowed parents to challenge the existence of local grammar schools and replace them with comprehensive schools had been rigged in favour of the former.

Another aspect of the government's education policy which raised concerns among party members was its introduction of tuition fees for higher education and its withdrawal of student maintenance grants. The government argued that the benefits of higher education were going disproportionately to the wealthier sections of society who should therefore make a contribution to the costs whilst ensuring that the poorest were excluded from these payments.

Crime and justice

The government pursued its objectives of cutting crime and anti-social behaviour by encouraging tough policing and sentencing policies and by proposing to restrict the rights of some accused to a jury trial. Curfew orders on young children and training of parents of constantly offending children were introduced and problem families on estates were evicted. In response to his critics, Jack Straw argued that their views were those of middle-class, 'Hampstead liberals' out of touch with the concerns and fears of working-class communities on council estates.

In contrast with the earlier Labour governments of the 1960s and 1970s, the extent and depth of criticism of the Blair government's policies coming from within the party was muted. The parliamentary Labour Party was less divided (Cowley and Stuart, 2001), and the NEC and annual conference were no longer the venues for well-publicized rows. The explanations for this harmony are twofold; first, as we will see in Chapter 6, the membership was broadly supportive of the government's programme. Second, as we will see in the next section of this chapter, the structural changes made to the party organization provided fewer opportunities for critics to mount any sustained public opposition.

Organizational reforms in the Labour Party

We have already referred in this chapter to the Labour Party's abandonment of its traditional commitment to delegatory democracy by 1997. This involved introducing ballots of individual members to select leading personnel and referenda to approve constitutional reform and endorse the 1997 election manifesto. These new balloting procedures were supplemented by reform of the party's policy-making procedures immediately after Labour was elected to office in 1997. The immediate impetus for the policy-making reforms was the leadership's desire to avoid the strained relationships between the party in government and the party outside government which had occurred on the occasion when Labour had last been in office. The new policy-making procedures, based upon a NEC report, *Partnership in Power* (1997), significantly modified the party's previous policy-making arrangements which had prevailed for more than 80 years.

Partnership in Power stated that the party's policy-making procedures were flawed because few members were able to participate and the motions discussed at annual conferences were unsatisfactory. The procedures should therefore be reformed to 'give more opportunities for a bigger cross-section of party members to get involved in the party processes and debates, widening their rights to engage in policy development through a more deliberative and extended procedure, without detracting from the sovereign powers of annual conference' (Labour Party, 1997b: 6). The report proposed the establishment of a joint policy committee, a national policy forum and eight policy commissions to replace the NEC and the annual conference as the formal sources of party policy. The joint policy committee was charged with the 'strategic oversight of policy development' (Labour Party, 1997b: 8), and the national policy forum with overseeing 'the systematic and continuous development of policy in the rolling programme' from which would be drawn the manifesto for the next election (Labour Party, 1997b: 10).

Eight policy commissions were established to cover foreign affairs, crime and justice, democracy and citizenship, economic affairs and social security, education and employment, the environment, transport and regions, health and, finally, industry, culture and agriculture. The membership of these commissions was composed of three representatives each from the government, NEC and national policy forum.

Formally the policies emerging from the policy commissions, debated within the national policy forum, and approved by the joint policy commission, still required the endorsement of the annual conference. *Partnership in Power* reaffirmed that '(a)nnual conference remains the sovereign policy- and decision-making body of the Labour Party' and therefore 'no statement would become party policy without being approved by Conference' (Labour Party, 1997b: 7). In practice, as the critics of these new structures claimed, the role of the annual conference as the sole arbiter of party policies had been downgraded.

In Figure 1.4 we display how these new structures were merged with the old. A two-year cycle of policy making was established in which in the first year the policy commissions would consult both within the party but also outside of the party with community groups, voluntary organizations and businesses on the priorities for policy development. Their reports at the end of the first year would

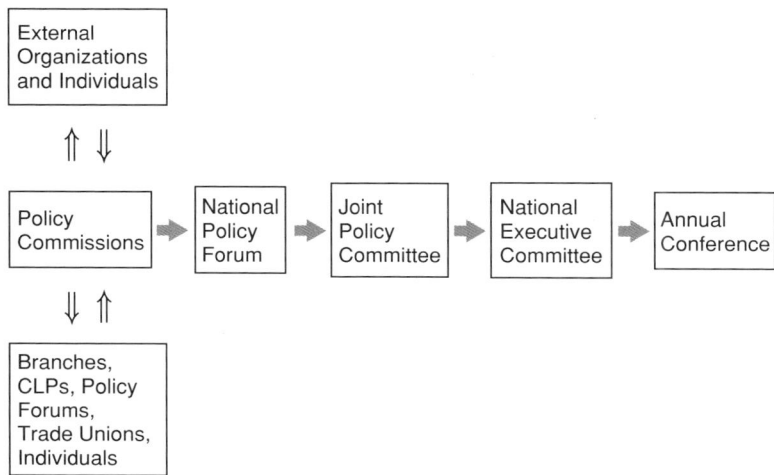

Figure 1.4 Labour's new policy-making system

be discussed, first, by the national policy forum and then by the joint policy committee, before being submitted by the NEC to the annual conference for further discussion

The second year of the cycle would be more formal and internal, culminating in draft policy documents to the national policy forum. After these policy documents had been agreed by the national policy forum they would be widely distributed through the party for formal consultation. Submissions and proposed amendments to the reports would be invited and policy commissions would then draw together their final reports to the national policy forum. The national policy forum report, which *Partnership into Power* suggested might include alternative proposals representing different points of view, would then be submitted to the conference for debate. By contrast with the past, when policy statements had 'been presented to Conference on an all-or-nothing basis', *Partnership into Power* proposed that with this new rolling programme 'Conference would for the first time be able to have separate votes on key sections and proposals in the policy statement' (Labour Party, 1997b: 15)

An important function of the annual conference in the past had been to act as a 'bellwether' of party opinion. Resolutions submitted for the conference agenda reflected the immediate concerns of all sections of the party and had therefore been one simple, if crude, means of assessing grassroots activists' opinions. Under the new procedures this would no longer be the case. Resolutions on subjects being considered by policy commissions would go directly to them and would therefore be excluded from the conference agenda. *Partnership in Power* claimed that the existence of policy commissions would mean that 'all year round there are bodies to which branches, CLPs, affiliated organisations can express views and concerns in all areas of policy and through which the party is able to have a continuous dialogue with government' (Labour Party, 1997b: 17). Whereas the annual conference agenda had been a very public reflection of grassroots' concerns the new procedures would be more discrete and private.

In order to try and meet the need for a safety valve for grassroots' immediate concerns, constituency parties and affiliated organizations would be able to submit one resolution to the conference on a topic not covered in the ongoing work of the national policy forum and therefore not addressed on the conference agenda, and conference delegates would vote to decide the priority of these emergency resolutions at the conference.

The immediate initiative for this transformation of party structures had come from the party's general secretary, Tom Sawyer. Reflecting on the changes after he had retired as General Secretary, Sawyer contrasted the old and new procedures in the following manner:

> ...out went motions, amendments and composite motions; and with them the sterile year on year debates about the same issues. And out went the stitch ups and the rows that always accompanied these procedures, which of course were heaven for the media. Instead, in came the detailed policy documents with a year round consultative period involving members and ministers, culminating in a final vote at conference once the consultations were complete. The result is a policy making process in which thoughtful and creative contributions count more than rhetorical table thumping. (Sawyer, 2000: 8)

To what extent is Sawyer correct in claiming a more thoughtful, creative and participative policy process? Have these new structures empowered the individual member? Has there been a dialogue between the membership and the party leadership in which the latter has responded to the former's opinions? Or, have the new structures strengthened the powers of the leadership? Since the structures are still in their infancy an assessment of their impact is inevitably tentative. Nevertheless all eight policy commissions have completed their three-year cycle of policy making and an election manifesto has been produced so it is possible to draw some immediate conclusions.

Before doing so we should point out that the modus operandi of all eight policy commissions varied quite considerably and for a complete answer to the question of their effectiveness they would all need to be examined separately in some detail. Our purpose in this chapter is not to provide a detailed study of intra-party power relations, but rather to assess the extent to which members have the opportunity to participate in policy making and the extent to which they are committed to these new structures and procedures. Our generalizations are therefore drawn with this in mind.

First, the small size of the national policy forum (175 members), and the fact that when it meets two or three times a year it meets in private, means that very many members are unaware of its existence and of its deliberations. This reduces members' sense of ownership of party policies. As Sawyer notes, 'it still only involves a small number of party activists, and those who are not involved feel distanced from the process' (Sawyer, 2000: 8). At least open and public disputes at party conferences over policies ensured that a good number of members were aware of the party's policies even if, on occasions, they disapproved of the party's particular stance.[4]

Privacy does have its advantages. It enables concessions to be made by the leadership with less likelihood of media accusations of weakness, defeat and climb-down. Meeting in private reduces the chances of adversarial confrontations and encourages a more consensual atmosphere. But privacy provides greater scope for manipulation: reports, agendas, minutes and debates, all in public, do not eliminate manipulation but they make it more difficult. For example, the workshop discussions at the national policy forum are guided by facilitators who then produce summary reports of the proceedings, which are the basis for the final statement. This gives considerable interpretative powers to facilitators who are often full-time personnel working in the party organization. Furthermore, a large part of the discussions at the national policy forum regarding amendments to commission reports are between ministerial teams and individual members of the national policy forum, and in such an environment it is possible for individuals to be isolated.

Evidence from our membership survey in 1999 revealed that between 35 000 and 40 000 members had participated in national, regional or local policy forums. Most certainly this is a greater number than participated in the party's previous policy discussions, which centred on branches and general committees of constituency parties. We discuss the member's reactions to the policy forums more fully in Chapter 6, but as a summary statement they have been a success for the participants, since most enjoyed the experience. However, only a minority among them believed such forums to be influential. The danger to the party is that members will regard them as uninfluential talking shops and will have little sense of policy ownership. Neither should it be forgotten that even with the participation of 10 per cent of the membership there is another 90 per cent, or 300 000 members, who have not participated.

Second, resources, particularly expertise, time and information, are distributed very unevenly in this new process of policy making. In meetings of the policy commissions and the national policy forum workshops and amendment sessions the party leadership has a huge advantage. Ministerial teams, with their advisors, inevitably dominate discussions and proceedings. In the preliminary discussions of policy documents at the national policy forum the imbalance of power between the well-resourced ministerial team and others has been very apparent. To some extent trade union representatives can call upon their own professional staff for support. So can the local government representatives. But the constituency party representatives lack such resources and even lack the knowledge acquired through collective organization. Moreover such information is difficult to acquire. For example, national policy forum members do not see the submissions coming into the eight policy commissions from the affiliated bodies.

Third, there are no bloc or weighted votes in the national policy forum, with 'one person, one vote' decision-making prevailing. So a trade union general secretary has the same clout as a constituency party representative. There is none of the inbuilt weighting of votes in favour of the trade unions that prevailed in the past, and still does to some extent at the annual conference. In that sense, the power of the trade unions relative to the constituency parties has been reduced quite dramatically. Nevertheless, as previously pointed out, trade unionists have access to resources and they also organize collectively and so their position within the national policy forum is still very strong.[5] Trade unions possess considerable potential to influence national policy forum outcomes.

One example of this can be cited from a forum meeting in Durham (July 1999), at a time of concern about the government's cuts to some welfare benefits and its refusal to link rises in pensions to rises in average earnings. An agreement between the party leadership and a few senior trade unionists to establish an enquiry into welfare provision resulted in trade unionists supporting none of the critical amendments which had been tabled about welfare provision.[6] As a consequence, the national policy forum report to that year's party conference presented a united face on welfare policy, because significant demands for reform had been eliminated from the debate.

Finally, there is the danger that these more consensual policy-making procedures can produce blandness and fudging of issues. Jeremy Beecham (2000), a prominent local government leader, has argued that disagreement and conflict is sometimes worthwhile because it helps to clarify policies and make them more meaningful. His comment on the NPF meeting in July 2000 was that 'the pressure to find consensus at the Forum was intense and I believe that we run the danger of producing muddled and unworkable policies in some cases – it would be better to resolve those arguments and for those who lose to accept the outcome.'

The new policy-making procedures do not facilitate either debate or accountability. For example, a commitment in *Partnership into Power* to minority positions being debated at the annual conference has been undermined by rules making such debate exceedingly difficult.[7] As a consequence, no minority positions were debated at the 1999 party conference and yet there were quite clearly issues in that year's NPF reports on health, justice, crime and welfare upon which members had expressed concern and did not share the leadership's point of view. Furthermore, attempts on the conference floor by those disagreeing with the reports to refer them back were met by outright refusal from the chair.

26 *The Blair Project: Setting the Context*

The remaining contextual issues which need to be addressed before focussing on the party members are the public's perceptions of Labour in power and the attitudes of backbench Labour MPs to the new government. We address these issues next.

Attitudes to the Blair government

There are three aspects to changing attitudes to the Blair government. These are the attitudes of the public, the attitudes of backbench Labour MPs, and the attitudes of party members. We examine the first and the second here since they are a background to our main focus, which is the attitudes of party members. We leave the discussion of the latter until Chapter 6.

The public

Throughout the first term of the Blair government the party maintained a high level of public support, as reflected in public opinion polls. The usual mid-term trough of public support for any government did not really occur. Figure 1.5 shows trends in Tony Blair's satisfaction ratings as Prime Minister and Labour voting intentions from the month after the 1997 general election to the month before

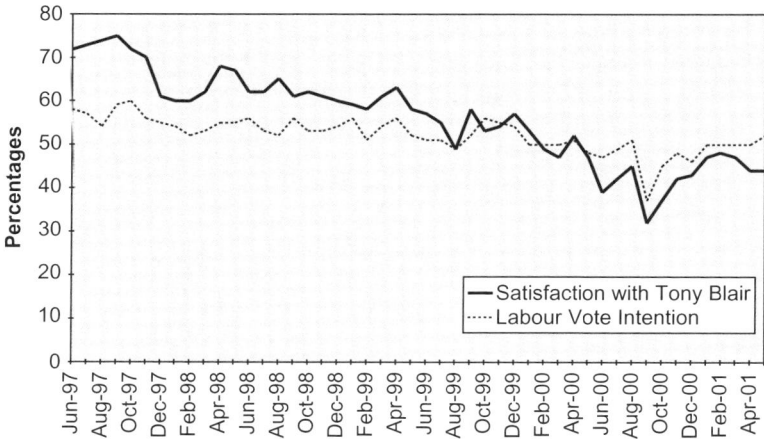

Figure 1.5 Tony Blair's satisfaction rating and Labour voting intentions, 1997 to 2001

Table 1.2 Labour's performance in elections in 1999 and 2000 (percentages)

	General Election June 1997	Scottish Parliament May 1999	Welsh Assembly May 1999	European Parliament June 1999	London Assembly May 2000	General Election June 2001
Labour	43	39	38	28	30	41
Conservative	31	16	16	35	29	33
Liberal Democrat	17	14	14	12	15	19
Nationalists	3	29	28	—	—	3
Others	7	3	5	24	26	2

the 2001 general election. It is interesting to note that voting intentions followed a trendless fluctuation, apart from the brief period of the fuel crisis of late 2000, and remained at a high level over time. In contrast, Tony Blair's satisfaction ratings declined more or less continuously, and only showed a modest recovery in 2001. Thus the Prime Minister's satisfaction ratings started well above the Labour voting intention series in 1997, but ended up well below it by 2001.

Labour's overall popularity was not reflected in elections to the devolved Scottish Parliament and Welsh Assembly, and the European Parliament, held in 1999 and to the London Assembly in 2000. In these elections the party consistently polled fewer votes than the opinion polls were predicting.

Finally, there is the result of the 2001 general election, which gave Labour a majority of 179 with a 41 per cent share of the vote. The remarkable election victory was set against a background of considerable policy dissatisfaction on the part of the electorate with Labour's performance in delivering its policy goals. According the British Election Study campaign survey conducted just prior to the election there was considerable discontent with Labour's performance on the National Health Service, education, and crime, as can be seen in Figure 1.6.

Respondents in the election study survey were asked to give the Labour government a score out of ten for its performance on these key issues, and it can be seen that the average scores were all below six, with ratings for the health service and for crime being particularly poor. Altogether some 51 per cent of the respondents gave the government a score of five or less for health and 54 per cent did this for crime. The same survey showed that some 53 per cent of respondents thought that the government had done a bad job or a very bad job in handling the foot and mouth disease crisis in 2001, indicating that policy discontent was widespread in the electorate.

Despite the evidence in Figure 1.6 the Conservatives were unable to exploit voter dissatisfaction with key spending areas like the health service, crime and education, because their priorities focussed on lowering taxes rather than on increasing provision. We discuss the implications of Labour's electoral victory in 2001 later, but for now it is clear that the party escaped the electoral consequences of its poor record of spending on public services at that election.

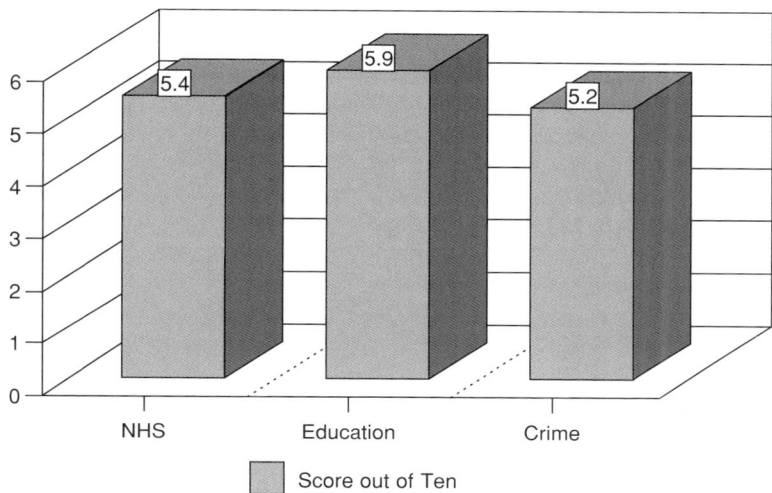

Figure 1.6 Mean scores out of ten for Labour's performance in handling public services, 2001

Labour backbench MPs

Labour governments of the 1960s and 1970s were faced with parliamentary revolts by their backbenchers. Since 1997, however, the Blair government has had few such problems. Even though there were some well-publicized revolts by groups of Labour backbenchers against government three-line whips on the proposed cuts in child benefits for lone parents (December 1997), the abolition of student maintenance grants (June 1998), and the proposed changes to incapacity benefits (May and November 1999), overall backbenchers, as can be seen in Table 1.3, exercised considerable party loyalty.

There are various explanations for this loyalty. They include the patronage powers of the party Whips and the strong New Labour inclinations of the new intake of Labour MPs, but Cowley and Stuart (2001) argue that strong support for the Blair government's policies in general is the most powerful reason for the absence of intra-party conflict at Westminster.

This strong underlying support for the government among its backbenchers was also reflected within the government itself. So, for example, no senior figures resigned from the government between

Table 1.3 Number of Labour backbench rebellions, 1964–2001

Years	Number of backbench rebellions
1964–1970	110
1974–1970	317
1997–2001	83

Source: Cowley and Stuart (2001).

1997 and 2001. Peter Kilfoyle, a junior Minister of Defence, resigned in January 2000 and expressed various criticisms of the government for not showing more concern for Labour's heartlands. In particular, he was concerned about the failure to increase the basic pension, for a tendency to blame the victim in the case of the unemployed, for discriminating in favour of Scotland, Wales and the South East of England, and for not developing a regional economic policy to help solve the huge problem of poverty in the northern regions of Britain (Kilfoyle, 2000). Even these criticisms seemed to be voiced more in sorrow than anger. No doubt they resonated among many party members but the overall impact of his criticisms was very short-lived at the time that he made them.

Overall, we can see that both the public and the parliamentarians were fairly satisfied with the performance of the 1997 to 2001 government. We now move to the main focus of this book – the attitudes, backgrounds and activities of party members.

2
The Grassroots Members: Who Are They?

> We need more members to ensure that we stay in touch with the hopes and aspirations of the people of Britain. (*Labour Party Centennial Report*, 1999, p. 40)

The recruitment and growth of the membership

The Labour Party's emergence as a fully-fledged participant in the British party system dates from 1918, the year in which it acquired a distinctive political programme and created a dues-paying, individual membership. By the 1940s the combination of both programme and large membership had established Labour as one of Europe's most important mass parties (Duverger, 1954). However, the Labour Party was never very serious about expanding its individual membership since it could rely upon the millions of trade-union affiliated members for money and resources. Furthermore, the development of new, mass communications techniques from the 1950s onwards, providing the chance to communicate directly with the public via television and advertising, encouraged the party leadership to pay even less attention to membership recruitment.

The party's long-standing indifference to membership recruitment changed after its massive electoral defeat in 1983. From then onwards leaders adopted a more proactive attitude to membership recruitment. As part of Neil Kinnock's strategy to restore the party's electoral support, he wanted to shift powers from the activists to the members but in order to do this he needed to recruit new members. Evidence of the party's commitment to membership expansion was the General

Secretary's promise in 1988, rash as it turned out to be, to recruit half a million members by the mid-1990s and one million by the end of the century.[1] However, few resources were devoted to membership recruitment and, therefore, although in 1989 the four-year downward trend in membership was arrested, the figures revealed a lower membership when Kinnock stepped down as leader than when he had first assumed the job. Furthermore, the Shadow Communications Agency, an important advisory body to the party's director of communications, Peter Mandelson, questioned the importance of party members in winning electoral support (P. Gould, 1998: 56). Kinnock might have wanted new members for political reasons, but his electoral strategists placed little importance on their role.

Nevertheless, at the 1992 general election the party's strategy of targeting those constituencies in which it believed it had a chance of winning seats, and which had involved extensive, long-term campaigning in them by using members to contact specific groups of voters, produced a demonstrable impact on election outcomes (Whiteley and Seyd, 1994). By the time that John Smith became the new leader his party had concluded (Labour Party, 1992: 68) that

> The evidence from the General Election results and the recent survey of party members clearly illustrate that there is a correlation between activity in the constituencies and the level of support for the party. The evidence explodes a long time held belief by some that local campaigning is of no great significance. It is therefore crucial that a greater part of our efforts has to be spent in giving support to local parties and individual members to revitalise and stimulate the party.

Smith reiterated his own strong commitment to members as both campaigners and ambassadors. Writing in *Labour Party News*, he stated: '... it is vital that we increase our membership. Members are the lifeblood of the party. From them flow ideas, campaigns, activities and income. And through them we can campaign on our policies and build local support for the party' (Smith, 1993). As a further inducement to the recruitment of additional, individual members Smith made a commitment that the relative weight of the trade union bloc vote within the party would diminish as the number of individual members rose.

His successor, Tony Blair, placed an even greater emphasis upon recruiting new members, albeit for rather different reasons, than his two predecessors. For Blair's New Labour project to attract voters he needed to demonstrate the party's newness and so undermine the Conservative's claim that 'old' Labour was lurking in the background. Newly-recruited members would assist him in this task. Perhaps of even greater importance was that new members, particularly if they were young and from a variety of class backgrounds, could be referred to as a demonstration of the party's modernity in contrast to Conservative traditionalism. Between 1994 and 1997 the number of individual members increased by 40 per cent, a considerable achievement given the prevailing assumption among many politicians, political journalists and academics that a mass-membership party was a feature of the past.

Figure 2.1 reveals, firstly, the fluctuating state of the party's membership between 1983 and 1994, then the considerable growth in the three years leading up to the 1997 general election and, finally, the drop in numbers since Labour was elected to government. We will return to the issue of membership in Chapter 7. Here we need to

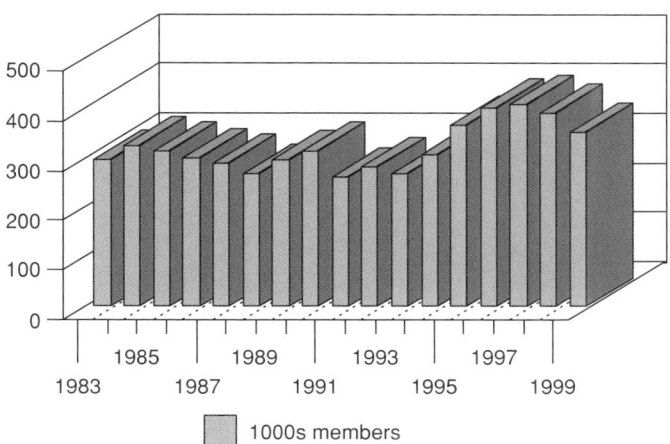

Figure 2.1 Individual party membership, 1983–1999
Source: Labour Party National Executive Committee Reports, 1984 to 2000.

stress the difficulty of obtaining accurate membership figures. Until the late 1980s the party was reliant upon the record keeping abilities of volunteers in constituency parties. Furthermore, for a long time local parties had reported unrealistically high membership figures because of the party's rule regarding the affiliation fees to be paid by local parties to headquarters. After 1980, however, membership figures became more accurate as, first, the affiliation requirement for local parties was eventually abandoned and, second, the party shifted in the late 1980s to a system of national membership record-keeping and, third, the time delay in allowing lapsed members to remain on the books was shortened to six months in 1999. Nevertheless, the single, annually-reported membership figure now issued from party headquarters needs to be treated with a degree of caution. We would want to stress that there is a constant flow of members into and out of the party and therefore the appropriate image is of the bathtub into which tap water is running but out of which water is running down the plughole.

In the remainder of this chapter we examine the demographic profile of Labour members in the late 1990s and whether this has changed much during the decade. We consider whether New Labour is an appropriate name, in the sense that it implies a new party with new members clearly distinctive from their pre-1994 colleagues. We will also compare Labour members and voters in 1997 and assess whether the party membership is demographically representative of the party voters. We begin by contrasting the personal characteristics of the members at the beginning and end of the 1990s.

A demographic profile of party members

Who now belongs to the Labour Party? In Table 2.1 we summarize some of the essential information about the social and demographic characteristics of the membership.

In the 1997 general election Labour's vote among women increased by 17 per cent and, for only the second time since 1945, the party attracted more than half the women voters in Britain (Norris, 1999: 152). Furthermore, 101 of the Labour *MPs elected* in 1997 (24 per cent of the total) were women. The party's aim of appearing more sensitive to women voters clearly paid electoral dividends in 1997. Nevertheless, this female-friendly strategy has not shifted the dominance of men among the members. Labour remains a male-dominated party at

Table 2.1 Socio-economic characteristics of the membership, 1990–97 %

	1990 (5032)	1997 (5757)
Gender		
Male	61	61
Female	39	39
Age		
25 & under	5	4
26–35	17	13
36–45	26	20
46–55	17	24
56–65	16	16
66 & over	19	23
Mean age	48	52
Occupational status		
Salariat	49	64
Routine non-manual	16	12
Petty bourgeoisie	4	2
Foremen & technicians	5	7
Working class	26	15
Trade union membership		
Yes	64	34
No	36	66
Education		
Graduate	29	34
Non-graduate	71	66
Type of employer		
Private sector	37	37
Public corporation	N/A	7
Other public sector	47	43
Charity/voluntary sector	N/A	9
Other	16	5
Ethnic origin		
White/European	96	95
Afro-Asian	3	3
Other	1	2
Strength of Labour partisanship		
Very strong	55	50
Fairly strong	38	43
Not very strong	6	6
Not at all strong	1	1

Table 2.1 (Continued)

	1990 (5032)	1997 (5757)
Religiosity		
Very religious	N/A	10
Somewhat religious	N/A	28
Not very religious	N/A	28
Not at all religious	N/A	34
Household income		
Under £5,000	17	8
£5,000 up to £10 000	21	17
£10 000 up to £20 000	33	25
£20 000 up to £30 000	17	19
£30 000 up to £40 000	8	12
£40 000 plus	4	19

its grassroots, with six out of every ten members men. For all Labour's attempts therefore to ensure that women have a prominent profile in the party, it has failed to shift the gender ratio and there are female members now arguing for internal party changes in order to attract more women into the party (Harman and Mattinson, 2000).

No party finds it easy to recruit young people as members. Only one per cent of Conservative members were 25 or under in 1992 (Whiteley, Seyd and Richardson, 1994) and only 2 per cent of Liberal Democrat members were aged 25 or under in 1999 (Seyd and Whiteley, 1999). Labour has only been slightly more successful in recruiting young people. In 1990 5 per cent of Labour members were aged 25 or under and seven years later the percentage had fallen to 4 per cent. Between 1990 and 1997 the overall mean age of Labour Party members rose from 48 to 52. The party has made attempts to reach young people via the youth organization, Young Labour, but this has not been very successful (see Table 2.1).

At the 1997 general election Labour's support among middle-class voters was higher than ever before. Using data from the 1997 British Election Study, Geoffrey Evans and his colleagues (1999: 91) state that 'the proportion of the middle class...voting Labour (was) far higher than at any previous point in the BES series'. Furthermore, they point out that 'the relative propensity of the working classes to vote Labour compared with the middle classes' had declined. This shift in the class composition of the party's voters is even more stark among its members. Using the Hope–Goldthorpe classification of occupations (Goldthorpe, 1980), the proportion of members in the salariat rose between 1990 and 1997 from one-half to two-thirds and, by contrast, the proportion classified as working class fell from one-quarter to one-seventh.

While we do not have demographic material on the party membership for the pre-1990 period which would help us to determine exactly when the class profile first began to shift in a significant manner, there are suggestions from local studies (Hindess, 1971; Forrester, 1976) that an upsurge in middle-class recruits occurred during the 1960s and 1970s. However, it is impossible from the data available to pinpoint precisely when the recruitment of middle-class members began to expand significantly. What we do have is survey data on those *leaving* the party in the early 1990s which helps us to answer whether those leaving the party were more likely to be working class than middle class. In 1992 we conducted a survey of members who had left the party in the previous year – that is, who had not renewed their membership in the previous year according to the records kept at party headquarters. This survey showed that 60 per cent of these exitors were members of the salariat and 17 per cent were members of the working class. Thus at this time middle-class members were more likely to leave the party than working-class members. Clearly had this trend persisted the party would have gradually become more working class. We can conclude, therefore, that the party must have been recruiting large numbers of the middle class in the mid-1990s.

Between 1990 and 1997 a dramatic 30 per cent decline occurred in the overall number of trade unionists among the members. Whereas in 1990 two-thirds of individual members had been members of a trade union, by 1997 the number of such party members had dropped to one-third. A study of party ethos (Drucker, 1979) suggests a dominant working-class, trade unionist culture. That, however, is very much the culture of the past. A contemporary study would not draw a similar conclusion. At its grassroots the Labour Party is now neither a working-class nor a trade union party.

With an increasingly middle-class membership it is more likely that members will be highly-educated. Other surveys show that among the three major parties the Liberal Democrats have the most highly-educated set of members, with 42 per cent of them being graduates (Seyd and Whiteley, 1999). By contrast, in 1997 one-third of Labour members were graduates, a slight increase over the seven-year period.

Much was made in the electoral studies literature in the 1970s and 1980s of the importance of sectoral divisions in explaining voter behaviour (see, for example, Dunleavy and Husbands, 1985) and it is certainly the case that Conservative and Labour members are employed in different sectors of the economy. So, for example, 60 per cent of Conservative and only 37 per cent of Labour members were employed in the private sector of the economy. Labour members have been drawn more from the public than the private sector. Over one-half (59 per cent) work or have worked in the non-profit sector of the economy, that is to say in central or local government, health authorities, universities, charities or trade unions. We should note, however, that, as a consequence of the structural changes to the British economy during the 1980s and 1990s, there are relatively more private-sector than public-sector employees in today's labour force.[2]

We have already referred to the fact that all British political parties find it extremely difficult to recruit young people as members. Similarly, all the parties experience enormous difficulties in recruiting members from among the ethnic minorities. Labour Party members have been and remain overwhelmingly white, with nine in every ten from a white, European background, and there is no evidence that this pattern of recruitment has changed in recent years.

Our first survey of members in 1990 revealed that at the grassroots the Labour Party was almost two distinct parties, one relatively well-off and the other relatively poor. This remains the case: one-quarter of the membership in 1997 had a household income of under £10 000 per annum while, in contrast, one-fifth had a household income of £40 000 and above. There were five times as many members with incomes in excess of £40 000 in 1997 than in 1990. While this finding can partly be explained by the effects of inflation, prices did not increase by such a high factor during this period. Consequently, there has been a clear increase in the real incomes of affluent Labour party members in this period.

Blair is the first Labour leader since George Lansbury in the inter-war years to be a strongly committed Christian and to draw a close link between his political and his religious beliefs. The Labour Party continues to attract both the believers and the non-believers: 10 per cent of members claimed to be 'very religious', while 34 per cent claimed to be 'not at all religious'. Blair's religious beliefs are established and high church, whereas historically the links between nonconformism and the Labour Party have been important. In contemporary times the nonconformists make up only 10 per cent of the membership, Roman Catholics 24 per cent, and the established church just over 50 per cent.

One of the reasons why parties recruit members is that they then have a group of partisans who, as well as being providers of time and money, are also loyal voters and supporters in both good times and bad. Nine in every ten Labour members retain 'very strong' or 'fairly strong' attachments to their party. What is noticeable, however, is that in 1997 party members were less likely to be very strongly attached to the party than in 1990. There could be a cohort effect here, with new recruits 'diluting' the strength of partisanship in the grassroots party. We examine this below. As Chapter 4 shows, strength of partisanship is an important predictor of participation in the party, so this is a development which could have serious long-term consequences for the party.

It is interesting to examine the extent to which individuals belong to the party out of a sense of collective or family identity. In our 1997 survey we asked members to tell us whether their parents, spouses and partners, where appropriate, are or were Labour members or voters. We see in Table 2.2 that where members had a spouse or partner, almost one-half of these (42 per cent) were Labour members and another 46 per cent were Labour voters though not members. So nine in ten of Labour members' partners or spouses were supporters of the Labour Party to differing degrees. In addition, members tend to come from strong Labour backgrounds: 16 per cent of their fathers and 12 per cent of their mothers had been Labour members and, in

Table 2.2 Family connections of members (percentages)

	Not Labour	Labour voter	Labour member	Labour activist
Spouse/partner	12	46	24	18
Mother	40	49	7	5
Father	38	46	7	9

addition, 46 per cent of their fathers and 49 per cent of their mothers had been Labour voters.

We now turn to an examination and comparison of the demographic profile of 'old' and 'new' Labour members, in other words those recruited into the party before and after Blair became leader.

'Old' and 'new' Labour Party members

> We have increased our individual membership by over one hundred and twenty thousand in a year and its now on its way to four hundred thousand. By the next election over one half of our members will have joined since the 1992 election. It is literally a new party. (Tony Blair speaking at the News Corporation leadership conference, Hayman Island, 17 July 1995)

Various claims, such as that made by Blair above, have been made regarding Labour's current membership. While Blair claims a new type of member but doesn't provide details of what he means, others have suggested that there was an influx of middle-class, inactive people into the party. For example, *The Independent* newspaper stated that the party's membership was 'increasingly middle class... (and) inactive' (4 January 1997), while the left-wing newspaper *Tribune* asserted that the new members were 'upwardly mobile yuppies, reminiscent of the old SDP, save that they now clutch mobile telephones rather than filofaxes' (28 July 1995). On a later occasion *Tribune* asserted that New Labour was perceived as 'metropolitan and middle class' (6 November 1998). Are such claims as these accurate?

In Table 2.3 we classify members as 'Old' and 'New' Labour. This refers to the date on which they joined the party, rather than suggesting any ideological predilections. Thus 'New' Labour members are simply those who joined the party after Blair became the leader in 1994, and 'Old' Labour are those who joined earlier.

We noted earlier the male imbalance in the party and this has grown slightly larger as a result of the influx of new members, since 63 per cent of the new recruits are male and only 37 per cent are female.

The ageing of members was modified slightly by the fact that Blair's party recruited more younger people. Among those recruited between

Table 2.3 The demographic characteristics of 'old' and 'new' Labour Party members (N = 5761)

	'Old' Labour (59%)	'New' Labour (41%)
Gender		
Male	60	63
Female	40	37
Age		
Under 18 years	1	4
22 up to 25 years	1	3
26 up to 35 years	10	18
36 up to 45 years	20	22
46 up to 55 years	26	21
56 up to 65 years	17	15
66 and over	25	17
Occupational status		
Salariat	67	60
Routine non-manual	12	13
Petty bourgeoisie	2	2
Foreman & technician	7	8
Working-class	13	17
Trade union membership		
Yes	38	29
No	62	71
Education		
Graduate	37	30
Non-graduate	63	70
Type of employer		
Private Sector	33	43
Public corporation	7	6
Other public sector	46	39
Charity/ voluntary sector	10	7
Other	5	5
Ethnic origin		
White/European	97	94
Afro-Asian	2	4
Other	1	2
Strength of Labour partisanship		
Very strong Labour	58	38
Fairly strong Labour	37	53
Not very strong Labour	4	9
Not at all strong Labour	1	1

Table 2.3 (Continued)

	'Old' Labour (59%)	'New' Labour (41%)
Religiosity		
Not at all religious	36	31
Not very religious	27	28
Somewhat religious	27	30
Very religious	10	11
Household income		
Under £5,000	8	7
£5,000 to £10 000	18	16
£10 000 to £20 000	24	28
£20 000 to £30 000	19	20
£30 000 to £40 000	12	12
£40 000 to £50 000	9	7
£50 000 to £60 000	5	5
£60 000 plus	7	5

1994 and 1997 there were three times the number of under 25 year olds and almost twice the number of 26 to 35 year olds as among the recruits joining before Blair became leader. Furthermore, the mean age of these new members (48) was six years younger than that of the long-standing members.

As we observed in Table 2.1, members of the Labour Party are overwhelmingly middle class. When we examine recruitment patterns during the 1990s we find, however, somewhat surprisingly, that the party recruited a slightly higher proportion of manual workers after 1994. Whereas one in eight members recruited before 1994 were manual workers, after 1994 the proportion shifts to almost one in six. This is surprising given Blair's tendency to downplay Labour's working-class and trade union roots.

One explanation of the recruitment of more manual workers between 1994 and 1997 is the determined attempts of some trade unions, for example UNISON, to encourage their political levy payers to join the party. However, this does not square with the fact that the proportion of trade unionists within the party fell among those recruited after 1994. Under Blair, the Labour Party distanced itself from the trade unions, believing that it would be penalized by the voters for too close a proximity, particularly in the light of the the disruptions in the public sector in the winter of 1978/9 and during the miners' strike of 1984/5. Indeed, in 1996 one shadow cabinet spokesman, Stephen Byers, was suggesting that the formal linkage between the party and the trade unions be broken. Among the newly-recruited members the proportion of trade unionists is low. The fact that more than 70 per cent of the New Labour recruits are not trade unionists is startling when it is recalled that membership of a trade union was a constitutional requirement for all individual party members until 1993. The abandonment of this rule helps in part to explain the decline. In addition, there are now far fewer trade unionists in the workforce (30 per cent of the total workforce in 1998) from whom to recruit party members. Nevertheless, the party leadership's attempts to distance itself from its traditional allies has clearly reduced any incentives that trade unionists might have had to join the party.

Just as we noted that there was a slightly higher proportion of manual workers among the newly-recruited members, so there were slightly fewer graduates among these new recruits. Of course, this trend is related to the increase in working-class recruitment to the party noted earlier.

Among newly-recruited members the preponderance of non-profit sector workers has declined in comparison with the past. New Labour contains many more private sector workers than does Old Labour. On the other hand there is evidence to suggest that the party has also had more success in recruiting ethnic minorities than in the past. Some 4 per cent of the New Labour recruits are from the African or Asian communities, compared with only 2 per cent of Old Labour members.

One striking development is the decline in the strength of partisanship among the New Labour recruits compared with the Old Labour recruits. Nearly 60 per cent of Old Labour members are very strong Labour partisans, compared with just under 40 per cent of New Labour members. As we shall see in Chapter 4 this has significant implications for the levels of activism in the grassroots party.

With regard to religiosity, there are only modest differences between the Old and New Labour members, and with regard to household income the former are slightly more affluent than the latter. Again, this is linked to social class, as extra working-class members tend to bring down the average levels of income in the party compared with the past.

We have already noted how under Blair's leadership the Labour Party reversed the decline in its membership that had taken place over the previous ten years. This was a significant achievement which contradicted the predictions of many political commentators. Did Blair succeed in recruiting members who were very much replicas of those already in the party? Or did he, in reversing the decline, break the mould of party recruitment?

His most striking impact was among younger people. Twice as many under thirty-five-year-olds were recruited after Blair became leader as compared with existing members. He clearly succeeded in motivating more young people to join the party. Secondly, he succeeded in attracting another group of traditional non-joiners, manual workers, although not to the same extent as among the young. Thirdly, Blair attracted more people working within the private sector of the economy into the party than had previously been the case. However, the one group of people among whom Blair's appeal was relatively unsuccessful was women.

We now move to another interesting aspect of the demographics of Labour Party supporters – the comparison between members and voters. This is particularly interesting since if the voters are very different from the members, the party runs the risk of losing touch with its electorate if it becomes too responsive to the demands of its grassroots members. Our party membership survey was conducted at approximately the same time as the British Election Study survey of voters in the 1997 general election which makes it possible to draw direct and valuable comparisons between members and voters.

Labour members and voters in 1997

Table 2.4 compares the demographic characteristics of Labour voters, using the 1997 British Election Study survey, and Labour Party members.

One of the most striking features of Table 2.4 is the gender imbalance between members and voters. In the 1997 election more than half of Labour's voters were women whereas, as we saw earlier, less than 40 per cent of members were women. This is one of the largest imbalances recorded in Table 2.4.

Labour voters are in general younger than the party members, although the differences in age are not great. The mean age of the

Table 2.4 Social characteristics of Labour Party members and voters (percentages)

	Members	Voters
Gender		
Male	61	49
Female	39	51
Age		
25 and under	4	11
26–35	13	19
36–45	20	20
46–55	24	19
56–65	16	15
66+	23	16
mean	52	47
Social class		
Salariat	64	26
Routine non-manual	12	21
Petty bourgeoisie	2	6
Foremen & technicians	7	8
Working class	15	39
Economic sector		
Private sector	37	67
Public corporation	7	4
Other public sector	43	26
Charity/voluntary sector	9	1
Other	5	1
Educational qualifications		
Graduates	34	9
Non-graduates	66	91
Household income		
up to £10 000	25	35
£10 000 up to £20 000	25	28
£20 000 and over	50	37

party's voters was 47 compared to 52 years for party members. However, whereas almost one in three Labour voters were under the age of 35, less than one in five party members were in this age group. At the other end of the spectrum, almost one-quarter of the members were aged 66 and over, compared with just one in six of the party's voters.

We have already pointed out that the party members are overwhelmingly middle class. Teachers in all sectors of education, social workers and public sector workers in general predominate among the membership. In stark contrast, manual workers were still the largest group of supporters among the party's voters in 1997, even though Blair succeeded in attracting more middle-class voters to the party than ever before. Two-thirds of members were in salariat occupations, compared to only one-quarter of Labour voters. There were proportionately two-and-a-half times more members of the salariat among the members than among Labour voters, and two-and-a-half times fewer manual workers among members than voters. Nevertheless, the party membership is slightly more representative of its voters in 1997 than ten years earlier. At the time of the 1987 general election there were three-and-a-half times more members of the salariat among party members than among voters, and one-and-a-half times fewer manual workers among members than voters (Seyd and Whiteley, 1992: 39).

Other interesting differences between party members and voters also exist. Over one-half of members are or were employed in the non-profit sector of the economy, such as health authorities, schools, universities, local authorities, charities or trade unions. By contrast, two-thirds of Labour voters are or were employed in the for-profit, private sector of the economy.

One-third of members were university graduates; by contrast, only one in ten Labour voters was a graduate. Finally, some 35 per cent of voters had household incomes of less than £10 000 per year, compared with 25 per cent of members. At the other end of the scale just over a third of voters had household incomes of more than £20 000, compared with 50 per cent of members.

Does it matter that in 1997 the social profile of the party's membership and voters differs in some very significant ways? Isn't it inevitable that the party elite and the mass of its supporters will differ? The gap may be inevitable, but it is important that it does not become too great. Party members are 'ambassadors' in local communities. As we shall see in Chapter 4, they often discuss politics with their friends and colleagues at work, so they are in a sense 'representatives' of the party.

Clearly, there is a danger that the mass supporters in the electorate will become less attached to the Labour Party if it appears to be represented by people who are different from themselves. Put simply, women in general, and unskilled blue-collar workers in particular, may have little fellow feeling with the male, affluent, educated members of the salariat. Arguably, they need constant cues and messages to support their attachments to the party, and if these appear alien then their identification with the party will atrophy. In this context codes of communication, including such things as language and dress, are important.

Most important are attitudes. Is the male, middle-class, highly-educated party elite sensitive to the needs and wishes of its mass supporters? Do they articulate their concerns? If the gulf is large, then it is likely that the mass support will diminish. This occurred in 1983 when the members were convinced that the party should pursue a policy of unilateral nuclear disarmament and extensive nationalization, but the party's supporters in the electorate were unconvinced. Historically the trade unions, as close party partners, have helped to bind their members to the party. Now, however, with that linkage weakened, and with some senior party personnel arguing that the links should be formally severed, this factor is less important. In addition, in the 1997 election the 'enemy' was a Conservative government which had been in office for 18 years. The existence of such an 'enemy' helped to mobilize mass support; but with Labour in office, the task of mobilizing mass support for the party becomes more difficult, as was seen in the 2001 general election.

It is this problem which has prompted debate about Labour's 'core' vote. It is claimed that the party's traditional supporters, namely manual workers and their families, will be less likely to vote for their traditional party in the future because it is abandoning its roots. In the 1997 general election Labour's vote declined in many of its safe seats. Since then, in European, Scottish, Welsh, local and parliamentary by elections there have been further signs of abstention among working-class voters. This trend was confirmed in the 2001 general election, when Labour's vote in its traditional heartland constituencies fell by more than its drop in the overall share of the vote (Seyd, 2001). The evidence for this is discussed more fully in the concluding chapter of this book, where we consider the implications of this latest decline in support from Labour's traditional supporters.

Since attitudes are the key to answering these questions, in the next chapter we turn to an examination of the extent to which attitudes have changed within the Labour Party during the 1990s, and consider whether these reflect the attitudes of its supporters in the wider electorate.

3
The Grassroots: What Do They Believe?

> 'New Labour remains a fragile project without deep roots'
> (*New Statesman*, 1 January 1997, p. 7)

We now turn to an examination of party members' political attitudes. In Chapter 1 we outlined some of the most significant policy shifts which occurred between 1983 and 1997 as the party attempted to revive its electoral support. Ian Budge (1999: 5) traces the policy shifts by examining the party's election manifestos from 1983 through to 1997 and concludes that the party moved to the right between 1983 and 1987, shifted to the left in 1992 (although to a less extreme position than in 1983), before moving significantly to the right between 1992 and 1997. Budge suggests that by 1997 Labour's manifesto positioned the party more towards the right than the Liberal Democrats.

Our purpose in this chapter is to assess the extent to which the positional shifts made by the party leadership in the 1990s have the support of the members. In particular, are the members part of the New Labour project? Can New Labour claim, as does Heineken lager, to reach down to all parts? Down at the party's grassroots do members support the idea of a 'third way'? Or do Old Labour ideas still linger? Have the ideas and policies identified with New Labour been imposed upon the party from above?

In our earlier study of party members (Seyd and Whiteley, 1992: 43–9) we suggested that they were attached to four socialist 'touchstones': public ownership, trade unionism, defence expenditure cuts, and high public expenditure. Do they remain as committed to these now? We will commence this chapter by, firstly, addressing this question. After that we will examine members' attitudes on a range of other issues; in particular, we will see whether they share the party leadership's views on electoral strategy and law and order policies, and the extent to which members have become post-materialists?

The question of Britain's membership of an increasingly integrated European Union is one that stimulates both inter- and intra-party divisions, and we will consider whether the Labour Party's shift towards a prominent pro-European stance in the early 1990s has been maintained in the face of a sustained campaign by parts of the British press to oppose this process of integration.

Throughout its life the Labour Party has contained distinct factions representing both the left and the right within its ranks. However, by the time of Blair's leadership the party seemed to be almost faction-free and in Chapter 1 we noted that the Labour government elected in 1997 experienced little of the factional opposition that had occurred during previous Labour governments. We will examine where members place themselves on the left/right party spectrum and, in particular, whether in Blair's Labour Party a cohesive left faction still exists.

Finally, in this chapter we will address the question of whether the opinions which members hold are representative of the party's broader band of supporters, namely its voters; and whether the opinions held by the party's activists differ in any significant manner from either the party's inactive members or its voters.

The political attitudes of party members

In 1990 members were in favour of public ownership and disapproved of the free market; they were attached to trade unionism; they wanted a reduction in defence expenditure and a defence policy which did not rely upon nuclear weapons; and, finally, they favoured high levels of public expenditure, even if this required increased levels of taxation. Do they still remain committed to these four socialist 'touchstones', none of which the party leadership would now want to be associated with? Are there any differences between newly-recruited and long-standing members with regard to these touchstones? Has the party recruited a new type of member since 1994 who is more committed to a New Labour programme?

In most of the following tables the first row gives the percentage responses of members surveyed in 1990. Then in the second and third rows we take our 1997 respondents and divide them into long-standing members (those who belonged to the party before Blair became leader in 1994) and newly-recruited members (those who joined the party between 1994 and 1997). It is this latter group who might be strongly attached to New Labour ideals. Finally, in the fourth row are the responses of all members in 1999. Thus the first and fourth rows measure changes in the attitudes of members over time and the second and third rows measure the differences between long-standing and newly-recruited members. (See Appendix for details of the surveys.)

There is little sign of members displaying any more positive enthusiasm for the free market in 1999 than in 1990. As can be seen in Table 3.1, just over one-quarter (27 per cent) agreed with the statement that 'The production of goods and services is best left to the free market', hardly any change since 1990, when 25 per cent agreed. However, over the nine-year period members certainly changed their minds on public ownership and became less enthusiastic. Whereas in 1990 82 per cent had wanted those publicly-owned industries which had been privatized to be returned to the public sector, by 1999 the figure had dropped to 50 per cent. And, in response to another question about nationalization, almost three-quarters (71 per cent) had desired 'more nationalization of companies' in 1990, but by 1999 the numbers preferring this option had dropped massively, to less than half (44 per cent). By contrast, whereas in 1990 only one-quarter (27 per cent) had supported the status quo position on ownership of leaving things 'as they are now', by 1999 this figure had risen to over one-half (51 per cent). By 1999 the majority of members believed that the structure of ownership in Britain, predominantly private, should remain that way. While members remained critical of the free market they were now no longer enamoured of public ownership in principle, although it is likely that there are particular industries, previously public utilities, which they would still prefer to see in public ownership.[1]

Did members differ in their views on the market economy and public ownership depending upon whether they were recruited to the party pre-or post-1994? The newly-recruited were more favourably inclined towards the free market than their long-standing colleagues:

Table 3.1 Members' attitudes on the market economy and public ownership in 1990, 1997 and 1999 (percentages)

	Year	Strongly agree	agree	Neither agree/ disagree	Disagree	Strongly disagree
(a) The free market	1990	5	20	17	34	24
	1997 Old*	3	20	20	41	16
	1997 New*	4	28	24	36	8
	1999	**3**	**24**	**19**	**39**	**15**
(b) Privatized industries	1990	45	37	10	7	1
	1997 Old	23	29	22	20	6
	1997 New	20	27	22	23	8
	1999	**18**	**32**	**23**	**23**	**4**

Statements:
(a) 'The production of goods and services is best left to the free market.'
(b) 'The public enterprises privatized by the Tory government should be returned to the public sector.'

		1997		
	1990	Old*	New*	1999

Are you generally in favour of:
- more nationalization of companies by government   71   52   44   44
- more privatization of companies by government   2   4   5   5
- or should things be left as they are now?   27   44   51   51

*As in Table 2.2, in all the following tables the terms 'Old' and 'New' are used purely to describe the dates on which members joined the party; anyone who joined before 1994 is defined as 'Old', and in 1994 and since as 'New'.

almost one-third of them (32 per cent), compared with almost one-quarter of long-standing members (23 per cent), believed that the production of goods and services should be left to the free market. Furthermore, long-standing members were twice as likely as newly recruited to 'strongly disagree' that the free market was best. Regarding privatization and nationalization, similar differences between the newly-recruited and the long-standing existed. A simple majority (52 per cent) of long-standing members expressed a preference for more nationalization as compared with 44 per cent of newly-recruited members and, by contrast, a simple majority (51 per cent) of new members preferred maintaining the status quo on ownership, as compared with 44 per cent of long-standing members.

While shifts certainly occurred in the entire membership's views of public ownership we should not lose sight of the fact that in 1997 nearly one-half of the entire membership (49 per cent) still desired more nationalization of companies by government. Who are these members who appear to be doggedly old Labour?

As we see in Table 3.2, there are some interesting variations in attitudes to public ownership, though none of them are large. Thus females are rather more in favour of nationalization than males; similarly, the young are more in favour than the older members. Both of these findings are surprising since it is often argued that women are less likely to be economic materialists, and the 18–25 generation received their early political education in the Thatcher years of privatization. Neither class, education nor, perhaps surprisingly, activism appear to relate to attitudes to nationalization. However, there is a clear distinction between the long-standing and the newly-recruited members, with the former more in favour of public ownership than the latter.

The second socialist 'touchstone' was attachment to trade unionism. In 1990, almost three-quarters of the membership (74 per cent) disagreed with the statement that 'it is better for Britain when trade unions have little power' and, as we see in Table 3.3, exactly the same percentage disagreed with this statement in 1999. A similar percentage of members (79) in both 1990 and 1999 believed that the government should not introduce stricter laws to regulate trade unions. Considering that, as we pointed out in the previous chapter, fewer than one-third of newly-recruited members belonged to a trade union it is surprising that there were not more differences between

Table 3.2 Members' attitudes to public ownership by gender, age, class, education, activism and year of recruitment in 1997 (percentages)

Are you generally in favour of:

	More nationalization	More privatization	Leave as now
All respondents	49	4	47
Gender			
Male	46	5	49
Female	54	2	44
Age			
18–25	54	7	39
26–45	53	4	44
46+	46	4	49
Class			
Salariat	49	4	47
Routine non-manual	51	2	47
Petty bourgeoisie	44	5	51
Foremen/technicians	46	4	50
Working class	51	4	45
Education			
Graduate	48	4	48
Non-graduate	51	5	45
Activism (hours per month)			
No hours	47	5	48
Up to 5 hours	52	4	44
More than 5 hours	52	3	45
Year of recruitment			
Old	52	4	44
New	44	5	51

newly recruited and long-standing members on this issue. Among newly-recruited members there were only slightly more who disapproved of trade union power than among long-standing members.

Members' third socialist 'touchstone' back in 1990 was defence and, in particular, a reduction in defence expenditure and an opposition to nuclear weapons. However, their commitment then was a response to 40 years of Cold War politics between the superpowers, an arms race and an increasing reliance upon nuclear weapons, all of which were just beginning to change at the time of our first survey. By 1999 their

Table 3.3 Members' attitudes on trade unions in 1990, 1997 and 1999 (percentages)

	Year	Strongly agree	Agree	Neither agree/disagree	Disagree	Strongly disagree
(a) Trade union power	1990	4	10	13	45	29
	1997 Old	3	10	14	49	25
	1997 New	4	13	19	48	17
	1999	2	11	14	46	28

	Year	Definitely should	Probably should	Doesn't matter	Probably should not	Definitely should not
(b) Trade union Laws	1990	3	9	10	29	50
	1997 Old	2	7	12	34	45
	1997 New	3	12	19	38	29
	1999	2	6	13	35	44

Statements:
(a) 'It is better for Britain when trade unions have little power.'
(b) The government should/should not 'Introduce stricter laws to regulate trade unions.'

Table 3.4 Members' attitudes on defence in 1990, 1997 and 1999 (percentages)

		Definitely should	Probably should	Doesn't matter	Probably should not	Definitely should not
(a) Defence expenditure	1990	60	26	3	7	5
	1997 Old	39	37	8	13	3
	1997 New	30	39	9	16	6
	1999	24	36	10	25	7

	Year	Strongly agree	Agree	Neither agree/disagree	Disagree	Strongly disagree
(b) British nuclear weapons						
	1997 Old	5	25	12	31	27
	1997 New	9	32	13	28	17
	1999	10	35	11	24	20

Statements:
(a) The government should or should not: 'spend less on defence'.
(b) 'Britain should have nuclear weapons as part of a western defence system.' (not asked in 1990).

views had changed considerably. For example, we see in Table 3.4 that the numbers believing the government 'definitely should' spend less on defence had more than halved, from 60 to 24 per cent. However, 60 per cent still believed that the government 'definitely' or 'probably' should spend less on defence (a drop from 86 per cent in 1990). Between the long-standing and newly-recruited members there were no significant differences of opinion.

In 1999 the membership was equally divided on whether Britain should or should not possess nuclear weapons. A similarly-worded question was not used in 1990 and therefore a direct comparison of opinions cannot be made, but in 1990 72 per cent believed that 'Britain should have nothing to do with nuclear weapons', suggesting again a major shift on this issue. Newly-recruited members were far more likely than their long-standing colleagues to agree that nuclear weapons should be part of western defences although even among the newly recruited a simple majority remained opposed.

Members' fourth and final 'touchstone' was a commitment to high public expenditure even if this required higher levels of taxation. In 1997 Blair and Brown had committed the party, if elected, not to raise personal levels of taxation during the lifetime of the next parliament, nor to alter the Conservative government's public expenditure commitments for the first two years of the next parliament. How far did members share the leadership's desire not to be identified as a 'tax and spend' party?

We see in Table 3.5 that whereas almost three-quarters (73 per cent) of the members in 1990 believed that the government should not reduce government spending by 1999 the number had dropped, but almost two-thirds (65 per cent) still remained committed to maintaining levels of government expenditure. The number of those believing that government 'definitely should not' reduce government spending had dropped from 44 to 27 per cent. But between 1990 and 1999 there was only marginal change in the percentages, less than one-quarter in both years, who believed that government spending should be reduced. So between 1990 and 1999, notwithstanding New Labour's attempts to divorce the party from a high public expenditure image, members retained a commitment to this traditional social democratic viewpoint.

On this issue the newly-recruited differed significantly from long-standing members: 36 per cent of the newly-recruited, in contrast to 26

Table 3.5 Members' attitudes on taxation and public expenditure in 1990, 1997 and 1999 (percentages)

			Definitely should	Probably should	Doesn't matter	Probably should not	Definitely should not
(a) Reduce government spending	1990		6	15	6	29	44
	1997	Old	4	22	9	38	27
	1997	New	6	30	11	36	17
	1999		**3**	**20**	**12**	**38**	**27**

	Year	Strongly agree	Agree	Neither agree/ disagree	Disagree	Strongly disagree
(e) High income tax	1990	13	22	11	38	16
1997	Old	5	16	13	49	17
1997	New	8	22	13	46	11
	1999	**7**	**23**	**13**	**43**	**14**

Statements:
(a) The government should/should not: 'Reduce government spending generally.'
(b) 'High income tax makes people less willing to work hard.'

per cent of the long-standing, believed that the government should reduce government spending. Nevertheless, an overall majority (53 per cent) of newly-recruited members still believed that the government should not reduce government spending.

As far as taxation is concerned, the story is a similar one. Members have not changed their views over time that high income tax is not a disincentive to work. In 1990 54 per cent disagreed with the statement that 'high income tax makes people less willing to work hard' and by 1999 this figure had risen to 57 per cent. More newly-recruited than long-standing members viewed high income tax as a work disincentive, but the majorities in both groups were uncritical of high income tax.

What is clear therefore from our surveys is that some shifts of opinion have occurred among members on two of the four socialist touchstones which we originally emphasized. Members feel far less strongly than they did that the government should reduce defence expenditure, although they still believe that expenditure savings should be made in this field, and they are far less committed to nationalization. However, they remain as sceptical of the market economy, as committed to taxation and public expenditure and as supportive of trade unions as they were at the beginning of the decade. So in response to our earlier questions regarding Old and New Labour we can say that support among members for the party leadership's rewriting of Clause IV of the party constitution to take out the commitment to nationalization is extensive. But at the grassroots support for collective intervention in the market, for redistributionary strategies and for strong trade unionism remained consistently strong during the 1990s and belies any notion of a successful New Labour takeover of the party.

The consequence of Labour's 18 years in opposition was that the party at all levels was forced to reconsider its political strategies, and the longer the party remained out of office the more compelling became its strategic deliberations. We now examine the members' attitudes towards these strategic questions.

Party strategy

Back in 1990, when members were first surveyed, the Labour Party had been out of national office for 11 years, and had been recently

Table 3.6 Members' attitudes on party strategy in 1990, 1997 and 1999 (percentages)

	Year	Strongly agree	Agree	Neither agree/disagree	Disagree	Strongly disagree
(a) Party principles	1990	25	36	12	21	7
	1997 Old	19	42	17	20	3
	1997 New	19	44	16	18	3
	1999	**15**	**44**	**17**	**20**	**3**
(b) Traditional values	1997 Old	5	27	12	42	14
	1997 New	5	33	16	39	8
	1999	**5**	**24**	**10**	**43**	**18**
(c) Middle ground	1990	19	38	10	22	11
	1997 Old	8	34	20	30	4
	1997 New	10	39	21	26	8
	1999	**6**	**31**	**18**	**37**	**8**
(d) Class struggle	1990	28	38	14	16	3
	1997 Old	11	30	25	28	7
	1997 New	7	26	30	29	8
	1999	**9**	**30**	**26**	**29**	**7**

Statements:
(a) 'The Labour Party should always stand by its principles even if this should lose an election.'
(b) 'The Labour Party has not moved away from its traditional values and principles.' (not asked in 1990)
(c) 'The party should adjust its policies to capture the middle ground of politics.'
(d) 'The central question of British politics is the class struggle between labour and capital.'

engaged in a major policy review. As we see in Table 3.6, members at that time were clearly of the opinion that their party should always stand by its principles even if these should lose it an election. Nine years later, and by now in government, there was little change to this viewpoint. However, members were not so certain that their party had stuck to its traditional values and principles. In 1999 a clear majority of 61 per cent disagreed with the statement that the party 'has not moved away from its traditional values and principles'.

Throughout the 1990s the party's electoral strategy was aimed at making the party more popular by appealing to moderate or centre-ground voters. Who exactly these voters were was clarified by Philip Gould, who defined them in the run-up to the 1997 election as 'aspirational' voters (Gould, 1998: 122). In the first flush of an overwhelming election victory in 1997 members seemed confident that enough of a move to the centreground had been made; whereas in 1990 57 per cent had wanted the party to 'adjust its policies to capture the middle ground of politics,' by 1999 this figure had dropped to 37 per cent. The number of members 'strongly' agreeing with a centreground electoral strategy had dropped by one-third. By 1999 a simple majority (45 per cent) disagreed with the statement. So the membership believed that the party had gone far enough in its centreground strategy by 1999.

Where we do see a very large shift in members' attitudes is with regard to class politics. In 1990 66 per cent of them agreed that 'the central question of British politics is the class struggle between labour and capital', but by 1999 the figure had dropped to 39 per cent. Furthermore, three times as many members 'strongly agreed' with this statement in 1990 as in 1999. So Blair's clear statement in a speech to the party's annual conference in 1999 that an ideology attached to class conflict was outdated and that there was a need for a new 'third way' had strong support at the grassroots.

On these strategic questions there are few differences between the long-standing and newly-recruited member. The only one in which there is a significant difference concerns this question of the class struggle. Whereas a simple majority of the long-standing members (41 per cent) still believed that the class struggle is the central question of British politics, this finding is reversed among the newly-recruited, among whom 37 per cent disagreed with the statement.

In Chapter 1 we noted that an important aspect of the Labour Party's policy repositioning under Blair concerned the question of law and order. The leadership was keen that the party should be identified more with the victims of crime than criminals and that policies should therefore be tough on criminals. Did members share the party leadership's desire to be seen as tougher on criminal behaviour?

Law and order

We see in Table 3.7 that majorities of the membership supported the fining of the parents of juvenile delinquents, for ensuring that those sentenced to life imprisonment remain there for life, and for imposing stiffer sentences upon law breakers. They are less supportive of fining parents of juvenile delinquents than they are for a stricter sentencing regime. But the tough policing policies initiated by Blair when he was shadow Home Secretary, and then put into practice by Home Secretary Jack Straw after 1997, have strong support among members. What is especially noteworthy is that newly-recruited members of the party were much stronger supporters of these tough policies than their long-standing counterparts.

Although members adopted a tough attitude on law and order policies, they were more tolerant on lifestyle and personal moral behaviour issues. For example, majorities were tolerant of homosexuality and ease of obtaining abortions. However, members believed that the government should discourage the growth of one-parent families. On this question a complete shift in members' views has occurred since Labour entered government. Whereas in 1997 a majority believed that the government should not discourage the growth in one-parent families, in just two years their opinions had been reversed. How does one explain this shift? All that we can suggest is that the government's reduction of single mothers' benefits in 1998 swung members' views, although considering the furore this move created within the Parliamentary Labour Party we doubt this.

We noted that newly-recruited members were tougher in their attitudes on law and order issues than their longer-standing colleagues, and we find that they were less sympathetic towards homosexuality and abortion, but less condemnatory of one-parent families than their long-standing colleagues.

Table 3.7 Members' attitudes on law and order and lifestyle in 1997 and 1999* (percentages)

	Year	Strongly agree	Agree	Neither agree/ disagree	Disagree	Strongly disagree
(a) Fine parents	Old	17	30	14	26	13
	New	24	35	12	22	7
	1999	**17**	**34**	**14**	**27**	**9**
(b) Life sentences	Old	23	28	15	26	8
	New	33	28	13	21	5
	1999	**27**	**26**	**15**	**25**	**8**
(c) Stiffer sentences	Old	20	26	27	20	7
	New	27	31	23	15	4
	1999	**20**	**32**	**26**	**17**	**4**
(d) Homosexual relations	Old	9	8	17	30	37
	New	12	9	20	28	31
	1999	**8**	**9**	**20**	**26**	**37**
(e) Abortions	Old	9	13	18	27	34
	New	11	16	20	27	27
	1999	**7**	**15**	**14**	**35**	**29**

Table 3.7 (Continued)

	Year	Strongly agree	Agree	Neither agree/ disagree	Disagree	Strongly disagree
(f) One-parent families	Old	10	22	24	31	13
	New	7	18	20	36	19
	1999	**20**	**36**	**20**	**16**	**8**

*None of these statements were used in our 1990 survey.

Statements:
(a) 'The Labour government should fine the parents of juvenile delinquents as a way of curbing youth crime.'
(b) 'Life sentences should mean life.'
(c) 'People who break the law should be given stiffer sentences.'
(d) 'Homosexual relations are always wrong.'
(e) 'The government should make abortions more difficult to obtain.'
(f) 'The government should discourage the growth of one-parent families.'

In response to those who criticized Labour's tough law and order policies, Straw often made the point that working-class families suffered disproportionately from criminal behaviour. It is they who were more likely to have their lives and property disrupted by criminality than the critics who, he claimed, were disproportionately middle class. In Chapter 2 we noted that party members are overwhelmingly middle class and therefore might be less supportive of these tough policies. Here might be an instance in which the preponderance of middle-class members leads to the party's grassroots being out of touch with the views of a crucial constituency of its voters. When we examine members' attitudes according to their class background in Table 3.8, we find very strong evidence to confirm its influence. Working-class members take a much more punitive attitude to crime than do middle-class members. For example, three-quarters of working-class members (76 per cent) believe that 'life sentences should mean life', as compared with 45 per cent of the salariat. Three times as many members of the salariat as the working class disagree with this policy. Here is an issue upon which an overwhelming number of middle-class members could influence the party into policies which fail to reflect its working-class voters' concerns.

We noted earlier in this chapter that members have abandoned that powerful symbolic myth of Labour politics, the class struggle between capital and labour. Does this suggest that members had become post-materialists, as defined by Inglehart (1977)? Inglehart has argued that late-twentieth century societies are divided less by traditional economic, class-based issues and more by lifestyle issues such as environmental protection and individual rights. To what extent are members post-materialists in the sense that they wish to discourage nuclear energy and agribusiness, to restrict the use of the motor car, and to encourage equal rights for women? And are these issues ones in which the newly-recruited members display distinct post-materialist commitments in comparison with their long-standing colleagues?

Post-materialism

We see in Table 3.9 that members remained overwhelmingly opposed to the development of nuclear energy, although the numbers of those

Table 3.8 Members' attitudes on law and order policies by class, 1997 (percentages)

	Strongly agree	Agree	Neither agree nor disagree	Disagree	Strongly disagree
All respondents	27	28	14	25	6
Class					
Salariat	19	26	16	31	8
Routine non-manual	32	35	13	16	4
Petty bourgeoisie	25	30	18	18	10
Foremen/technicians	44	35	7	11	3
Working-class	46	30	11	10	3

Statement: 'Life sentences should mean life.'

Table 3.9 Members' attitudes on post-material issues in 1990, 1997 and 1999 (percentages)

	Year	Strongly agree	Agree	Neither agree/disagree	Disagree	Strongly disagree
(a) Nuclear energy						
	1990	4	9	8	36	44
1997	Old	3	10	19	41	27
1997	New	4	14	21	39	22
	1999	3	10	21	38	29
(b) Women's rights						
1997	Old	4	13	15	41	28
1997	New	4	14	16	43	23
	1999	5	14	15	42	25
(c) Modern farming						
	1990	44	41	10	4	0
1997	Old	31	47	15	6	1
1997	New	30	45	17	7	1
(d) Food versus countryside						
	1990	6	15	19	44	17
1997	Old	4	14	21	48	13
1997	New	4	13	20	49	14
(e) Higher car taxes						
1997	Old	16	42	13	21	7
1997	New	16	35	14	25	9
	1999	11	32	15	27	14

(a) 'Further nuclear energy development is essential for the future prosperity of Britain.'
(b) 'Labour should place less priority on achieving equal rights for women.' (not asked in 1990)
(c) 'Modern methods of farming have caused great damage to the countryside.'
(d) 'If farmers have to choose between producing more food and looking after the countryside, they should produce more food.'
(e) 'For the sake of the environment car users should pay higher taxes.' (not asked in 1990)

'strongly' opposed have declined significantly during the decade. No doubt the association of nuclear energy with nuclear defence commitments during the Cold War years intensified opposition to nuclear energy.

In Chapter 2 we pointed out that men predominate among party members. Nevertheless, less than one in five of the entire membership wanted the party to give 'less priority' to the achievement of equal rights for women. Two-thirds of the members disagreed with any party strategy of giving less priority to the achievement of equal rights to women and this remained consistent throughout the decade. Interestingly enough, there were significant gender differences in attitudes to women's rights. While 63 per cent of men disagreed with the idea of giving these rights a lower priority in 1997, this was true for 75 per cent of women members.

Since Labour came to office in 1997 an active rural lobby, organized primarily by the Countryside Alliance, has emerged to champion the countryside and to articulate views on a range of issues including foxhunting, rural transport, beef production, green-belt planning laws, and the growth of genetically-modified crops. The Countryside Alliance claimed that Labour was an urban party insensitive to the concerns of country people. Labour Party members were certainly critical of the way in which agriculture has developed in Britain. Over three-quarters of them in 1990 and 1997 believed that 'modern methods of farming have caused great damage to the countryside' and almost two-thirds believed that farmers should be more concerned with looking after the countryside than with producing more food.

The most serious damage to the Labour Party's popular support since the 1997 general election came from the protests of the fuel lobby to the rises in fuel taxes in September 2000. The vehicle-owning public is a large group of voters with the potential to be a powerful veto group on government policies. Certainly the government proceeded very cautiously in its policies to curb use of the motor car and this was reflected among the members. In 1999 they were almost equally divided between those wanting and not wanting to curb the use of the motor car.

Therefore, the answer to our question of whether a new politics of post-materialism has emerged among Labour's grassroots is that we find nothing new during the 1990s. Members have been concerned with such issues throughout the decade. Furthermore, in answer to our second question of whether a generational factor is at work among the members on these issues we find that there are no major differences in the standpoints of those recruited into the party pre- and post-1994.

Europe

One political issue which has consistently divided both Conservative and Labour parties over the past four decades has been the question of Britain's membership of, first, the European Community and, then, the European Union. Both parties have shifted their positions and both have found it difficult to maintain internal party unity. Although by the mid-1990s Labour had shifted to a strongly pro-EU standpoint, the Labour government was aware of hostile public opinion towards the EMS in particular and the EU in general which the Conservative Party sought to exploit. As a consequence, the Labour leadership positioned itself so as not to enable its political opponents to brand it as too pro-European. To what extent did the membership display pro- or anti-EU sentiments?

In 1990 when members were asked whether they wanted Britain to remain a member of the European Economic Community or to withdraw nine out of ten preferred membership. In 1997 when we last asked members for their opinion of withdrawal or not their preference remained overwhelmingly in favour of membership of the European Union. In Table 3.10 we go beyond the question of membership of the EU to see what their views were on further integration of the European Union and the introduction of a European common currency.

Two-thirds of the membership (67 per cent) in 1999 did not agree that 'Labour should resist further moves to integrate the European Union', only a slight reduction in the 1990 figure. Furthermore, one-half of the membership (53 per cent) believed that 'Britain should agree to the introduction of a common European currency'. So at a time when public opinion is hostile to the EU, the pro-European stance is strong among members and runs right through the party, with no significant differences between long-standing and newly-recruited members.

Factionalism has been a permanent feature of the Labour Party during most of the twentieth century and at times both left and

Table 3.10 Members' attitudes on Europe in 1990, 1997 and 1999 (percentages)

	Year	Strongly agree	Agree	Neither agree/disagree	Disagree	Strongly disagree
(a) Resist Europe						
	1990	5	11	13	48	24
1997	Old	4	10	12	49	25
1997	New	6	12	15	44	24
	1999	**6**	**12**	**14**	**42**	**25**
(b) Agree common currency						
1997	Old	17	41	24	15	11
1997	New	16	35	24	15	11
	1999	**19**	**39**	**22**	**12**	**9**

Statements:
(a) 'Labour should resist further moves to integrate the European Union.'
(b) 'Britain should agree to the introduction of a common European currency.' (not asked in 1990)

right have had an organized presence within the party. The balance of power within the party has always tended to favour the right and, as a consequence, it has been the left which has been more organizationally prominent. The history of the Labour left since the late 1960s was one of slow emergence into a powerful position by the late-1970s, followed by fragmentation and collapse in the 1980s and 1990s. By the mid-1990s the left had been marginalized within the party, and during the subsequent Labour government its organizational and programmatic presence was almost negligible. A recent analysis of the Labour left concludes that 'in the space of less than a decade, the Labour Left mutated from a powerful constituency of grassroot radicals capable of exerting remarkable leverage over the entire party, into a small, isolated and increasingly direction-less scattering of Labour traditionalists' (Young, 2000: 269). To what extent, however, does the left retain a presence among the hearts and minds of members?

In Table 3.11 we examine members' self-placement on a party left/right scale ranging from one to nine. In 1990 the mean position of members was 4.3 and in 1999 it remained similar at 4.2. When we contrast the mean position of long-standing and newly-recruited members we see only a slight difference between the two, with the new recruits marginally more right inclined.

We have already examined the characteristics of the members who believed in further public ownership to see whether they formed a distinctive group within the party. We concluded that little distinguished them from other members apart from the fact that women in particular, and among men and women, those under the age of 25, were more likely to be in favour of nationalization. If we now take the 15 per cent of the members who placed themselves in categories 1 or 2 on the left/right scale in 1999, in other words those who regarded themselves as on the very left of the party, they also have no distinctive, distinguishing characteristics from other members of the party. Neither their class, age, gender, education nor level of activism is in any way significantly different from the rest of the party membership. In other words, those on the left are randomly distributed among the 360 000 members.

Up to this point we have been discussing attitudes within the party, but there is the broader question of the relationship of members to the wider electorate. Are members' attitudes highly unrepresentative

Table 3.11 Members' self-placement on a left/right scale in 1990, 1997 and 1999 (percentages)

	1	2	3	4	5	6	7	8	9	Mean
1990	9	9	22	19	20	7	6	3	7	4.3
1997 Old	9	10	24	19	19	8	6	2	3	4.1
1997 New	5	7	18	19	25	10	10	13	3	4.6
1999	8	7	24	20	22	8	6	3	2	4.2

of Labour voters? If so, this has important implications for party strategy. We examine this issue next.

Labour members, activists and voters

We have already pointed out that a section of the membership, the salariat, held views on sentencing criminals which were at odds with the views of working-class members. This highlights what might be a more general issue – namely that the members, preponderantly middle class, might be out of step with the party's more working-class voters. To what extent do the members articulate opinions which are unrepresentative of the voters? This was the problem for the party in the early 1980s when the membership held views, on nuclear defence in particular, which were out of step with Labour voters.

In Chapter 2, we compared Labour voters identified in the 1997 British Election Study with our own 1997 survey of Labour members, and we do so again here. The British Election Study and the party members' survey contained a range of common questions which enables us to compare the two groups' political attitudes.

Table 3.12 contains indicators of the attitudes of party members, activists and Labour voters on a very broad range of similar issues covering economic, social and foreign affairs. When comparing members and activists we see that there are wide levels of agreement between the two groups, except that activists tend to hold their views more intensely than members.[2] For example, 60 per cent of members and 69 per cent of activists believed that the government should definitely spend more money to get rid of poverty. Similarly, 46 per cent of members and 56 per cent of activists believe that the government definitely should give workers more say in the workplace.

When comparing members with voters, we see that, apart from education and aid to poor countries, the members are more intense in their attitudes than voters, although again there is common ground of agreement between the two groups. For example, 84 per cent of members oppose the growth of private medicine and this is true for only 60 per cent of voters. Similarly, 73 per cent of members and 63 per cent of voters favour spending less on defence. One case, which is surprising, relates to attitudes to the redistribution of income and wealth. In this case voters are more radical than either

Table 3.12 A comparison of Labour Party members' and voters' attitudes in 1997 (percentages)

		Definitely should	Probably should	Doesn't matter	Probably should not	Definitely should not
Private education	Members	27	27	22	18	6
	Voters	10	17	34	26	14
Relieve poverty	Members	60	35	2	3	1
	Voters	71	25	2	1	1
Private medicine	Members	2	6	8	30	54
	Voters	8	16	16	35	25
National Health	Members	75	23	1	1	—
	Voters	87	11	1	1	1
Less defence	Members	35	38	8	15	4
	Voters	26	37	11	21	6
Trade union laws	Members	2	9	15	36	38
	Voters	9	21	20	29	20
Work place consultation	Members	46	45	6	2	1
	Voters	38	45	7	8	2

The question wording was: 'Please indicate whether you think the government should or should not do the following things, or doesn't it matter either way?'

- Get rid of private education
- Spend more money to get rid of poverty
- Encourage the growth of private medicine
- Put more money into the National Health Service
- Spend less on defence
- Introduce stricter laws to regulate trade unions
- Give workers more say in the places where they work

		Strongly agree	Agree	Neither agree nor disagree	Disagree	Strongly disagree
Overseas aid	Members	17	43	21	15	4
	Voters	7	31	23	30	11
Income	Members	23	44	20	11	3
Redistribution	Voters	30	46	15	8	2
Life	Members	27	28	14	24	6
sentencing	Voters	55	33	5	6	1
Citizen of	Members	31	29	23	13	4
Britain	Voters	42	36	12	9	1

Statements:
'The government should give more aid to poor countries in Africa and Asia.'
'Income and wealth should be redistributed to ordinary working people.'
'Life sentences should mean life.'
'I would rather be a citizen of Britain than any other country of the world.'

Tax and public expenditure

	Reduce taxes and spend less	Same taxes and spending	Increase taxes and spend more
Members	1	13	87
Voters	2	16	80

'Suppose the government had to choose between the following three options. Which do you think it should choose?'

- Reduce taxes and spend less on health, education and social benefits.
- Keep taxes and spending on these services at the same level as now.
- Increase taxes and spend more on health, education and social benefits.

members or activists, with 30 per cent of them strongly agreeing with redistribution, compared with 27 per cent for activists and 23 per cent for members. This may reflect the members' willingness to adjust their policy preferences in line with New Labour electoral strategy after four defeats in general elections.

Overall, with a few exceptions, activists are more intense in their attitudes than members who are in turn more intense than voters. The one issue where there is a fundamental disagreement between members and activists on the one hand and voters on the other is in relation to the abolition of private education. By and large, members and activists favour this, whereas the voters do not.

It used to be argued that party activists were extreme in their attitudes in relation to voters, but there is little evidence to support this view in the data. The motivation behind most of the organizational reforms which the party had introduced since 1983, which we discussed in Chapter 1, has been the view that activists were unrepresentative of the wider membership and that therefore members should be empowered at the expense of the activists. However, the evidence gathered in our surveys does not support this view.

This concludes our discussion of the attitudes and beliefs of party members and activist. In the next chapter we go on to examine their activities.

4
What Do They Do?

In earlier work (Seyd and Whiteley, 1992; Whiteley, Seyd and Richardson, 1994) we have identified three different aspects of political participation in parties. These three aspects are contact, campaigning and representation. The first of these concerns the levels of contact between party members inside the party organization, but also between members and the wider community. The second involves preparation for elections and actually running election campaigns at the local level. Occasionally members get involved in campaigns on issues which are not directly related to election campaigns, such as local campaigns designed to recruit new members. The third involves representing the party, both within the party organization as a constituency secretary or ward chairperson, and also on outside bodies either as elected representatives on the local council, or as representatives of the party on local organizations such as the area health authority or the magistrates' bench.

We will add a fourth dimension to this list, namely, giving money to the party. We have previously regarded this type of activity as one aspect of campaigning, and as the evidence below shows it plays an important role in election campaigning. However, it should be examined separately since recent empirical work on voluntary organizations shows that 'credit-card' membership is increasingly a feature of participation in modern Britain (Maloney and Jordan, 1997; Maloney, 1998). This refers to the phenomenon that participation for many people is limited to donating money to their favourite organization, and otherwise doing little else. Maloney (1998) speculates that for some individuals this might be a way of subcontracting their involvement to other people. In effect they are paying someone else to participate on their behalf. Accordingly, we examine this aspect of participation separately.

There is a common image of party members as people who sit in smoke-filled rooms debating complicated resolutions and following arcane procedures, but this is really a caricature of party activity. Indeed attending meetings is only one of a variety of activities undertaken by members as they work to keep the party organization going at the local level. In this chapter we examine each of these aspects of party activity in turn, looking both at the contemporary situation, and also at how these matters have evolved over time. This leads into a discussion of the factors which determine party activity at the individual level and helps to explain why some members are active when others are not.

The contact dimension of activity

The contact dimension refers to interactions between party members within the organization and also the role of members in representing the party to the outside world as 'ambassadors in the community' (Scarrow, 1996). Recent work shows that face-to-face political communication between individuals plays a very important role in democratic politics. Popkin (1991) has argued that in American politics, face-to-face communication between individuals helps voters to validate the political information which they receive about candidates for office or political issues. They are unlikely to take political messages at face value unless it is validated in this way, most commonly by someone who they know and trust. Lupia and McCubbins (1998) have also argued that trust is an essential requirement if individuals are to believe the political messages they receive. Since electors are much more likely to trust a friend or a member of their family than a stranger or an impersonal source in the media, this type of communication helps to make democracy work. For these reasons the role of party members as channels of communication between the party leadership and the wider electorate has been underestimated in the past.

Obviously highly active party members are likely to have a lot of face-to-face contact with each other at the local level, but it would be a mistake to think that contact is synonymous with activism. It is quite possible, for example, for members to be relatively inactive but to have regular contact with other members either socially, through their families, or because activists call on them to donate money, to sign petitions, to remind them to vote on election day, or to collect their membership subscriptions. Clearly contact is a necessary but not sufficient condition for activism.

Three key aspects of the contact dimension over the nine-year period of the surveys are measured in Table 4.1. There has been a dramatic decline in contacts between party members within the organization during this period. The proportion of members having no contact at all has nearly doubled over this period and the numbers having frequent contact has dramatically declined. A similar picture emerges in relation to attending meetings, an important indicator of contact which is often used as key measure of political activism. The proportion of the members who have attended no meetings at all in the previous year nearly doubled between 1990 and 1999, from 36

Table 4.1 The contact dimension of party activism (percentages)

'Thinking back over the last year, how often have you had contact with people active in your local branch or constituency party?'

	1990	1997	1999
Not at all	10	15	19
Rarely	17	19	20
Occasionally	29	33	32
Frequently	44	34	29

'Thinking back over the last year, how often have you attended a party meeting?'

Not at all	36	54	61
Rarely	14	16	9
Occasionally	20	10	12
Frequently	30	19	18

'Are you satisfied or dissatisfied with the level of contact from your local Labour Party?

Very satisfied	—	24	18
Satisfied	—	46	47
Neither	—	22	27
Dissatisfied	—	6	6
Very dissatisfied	—	2	3

per cent to 61 per cent. By the same token the proportion of members who frequently attended a meeting has almost halved. The frequent meeting attenders are the people who keep the party organization running between elections.

The third sub-table in Table 4.1 shows that even though contact between the members has declined sharply there is not much evidence of dissatisfaction with this state of affairs in the grassroots party organization. In 1997 some 70 per cent were satisfied with the level of contact, and this declined only slightly, to 65 per cent, by 1999. So despite the lower rates of contact between party members there is no great pressure to change this state of affairs.

A commonly heard argument is that members do not want to be stuck in long boring meetings involving dull organizational matters and this may be the explanation for the decline in attendance at meetings observed in Table 4.1. However, this is not so, as the evidence in Table 4.2 makes clear. This evidence suggests that members who attend meetings have fairly favourable impressions of them. By large margins, they found meetings to be interesting, friendly, efficiently run, united and easy to understand, and there were no discernible trends in their attitudes over time. On the other hand they

Table 4.2 Members' attitudes to party meetings (percentages) (members attending at least one meeting in the previous year)

Percentages thinking that the meeting was very or fairly:	1990	1997	1999
Interesting	71	72	71
Friendly	72	75	75
Efficiently run	70	66	67
United	60	62	59
Easy to understand	76	71	75
Left-wing	35	30	30
Modern	39	33	33
Boring	20	18	18
Unfriendly	16	13	13
Badly run	19	19	18
Divided	25	19	20
Hard to understand	11	11	6
Right-wing	20	13	14
Old-fashioned	29	29	21

were more divided on the question of whether meetings were left-wing or right-wing and on the question of whether meetings were modern or old-fashioned. But, overall, the evidence in Table 4.2 provides few grounds for arguing that members are discontented with meetings or for the argument that this dissatisfaction is the reason why their levels of contact with the party have declined.

The external contacts of party members with the wider society are examined in Table 4.3. This was a topic that we investigated for the first time in 1999 and so there is no earlier data relating to this issue. What emerges from the evidence in Table 4.3 is that party members are fairly efficient ambassadors in relation to the people they know, either as friends or as work colleagues. No less than 86 per cent of them talk about politics to people who are not party members, and clear majorities are asked for their political opinions by friends and by work colleagues, both of whom are very likely to know that they are Labour Party members. The only area in which they are reluctant to act as ambassadors is in relation to giving their political opinions to work colleagues without being asked. They are happy to do this with friends, but much more reluctant with work colleagues.

A large number of members who are willing to put the 'Labour' point of view in the community and in the workplace is an important resource for the party which has not fully been recognized in the past. This is particularly true in a context in which the print media is often politically biased and the electronic media has to pay close attention to party balance in its coverage of politics. Large numbers of party

Table 4.3 Contacts of members with individuals outside the party (1999) (percentages)

	Yes	No
Do members talk about politics with people who are not party members?	86	14
Do their friends ask for their opinions on political issues?	72	28
Do work colleagues ask for their opinions about a political issue?	51	48
Do they offer their opinions to friends without them asking?	56	44
Do they offer their opinions to work colleagues without them asking?	39	61
Do their friends know that they are Labour Party members?	91	9
Do their work colleagues know that they are Labour Party members?	71	29

members can play a very important role in getting the party message across to people in the community, assuming, of course, that they agree with it.

If contact is important then the campaigning dimension of participation is perhaps even more important and it is to this aspect that we now turn.

The campaigning dimension of activity

The campaigning dimension refers to a number of different activities, including fund-raising, organizing membership recruitment drives, arranging meetings, and running local election campaigns. For a general election, the 'long campaign', or the 18 months prior to a general election, is particularly important (Miller et al., 1990). The work of the general election campaign itself is relatively short, typically five or six weeks, but it is also very intensive. First, we examine generalized campaigning, before focussing more closely on campaigning in the 1997 general election in the next chapter.

The generalized campaigning measures in Table 4.4 relate to activities over the previous five-year period. The most striking development in this type of campaigning between 1990 and 1999 has been the decline in all types of campaign activities, with the exceptions of donating money to party funds and canvassing by telephone.

The largest decline in activities relates to attending meetings; more than two-thirds of members frequently or occasionally attended party meetings in 1990 and by 1997 this had fallen to under one-half. In

Table 4.4 Campaigning in the previous five years by members, 1990 to 1999

Percentage of members who frequently or occasionally did the following over the previous five years:	1990	1997	1999
Displayed an election poster in a window	86	78	76
Signed a petition supported by the party	89	65	60
Donated money to Labour Party funds	66	70	68
Helped with party fund-raising	—	35	34
Delivered party leaflets during an election	77	59	61
Attended a party meeting	68	46	48
Canvassed door-to-door on behalf of the party	55	31	32
Canvassed voters by telephone	—	10	13

Table 4.5 Members' perceptions of the effectiveness of campaign activities

Percentage who think that the following activities are very effective or effective:	1990	1997
Displaying an election poster in a window	67	76
Donating money to Labour Party funds	87	92
Delivering party leaflets during an election	87	83
Attending a party meeting	63	43
Canvassed door-to-door on behalf of the party	89	81

addition there were significant declines in the important election-related activities of delivering leaflets and doorstep canvassing over this period. In relation to door-to-door canvassing, the increasing importance of telephone canvassing in campaigns might explain some of the decline in the member's willingness to knock on doors.

One reason for this development is that members may have decided that some or all of the campaigning activities listed earlier are not very effective in helping the party to achieve its goals. However, the evidence in Table 4.5, which examines members' perceptions of the effectiveness of campaign activities, suggests that this is only really true for meeting attendance. As far as the important election-related activities of door-to-door canvassing and leafleting are concerned, there is no evidence to suggest that members increasingly see them as ineffective. Clearly, therefore, this cannot be the explanation of the decline in these activities over time.

However, in the case of attending meetings there has been a significant decline in perceptions that they are an effective way for the party to achieve its goals. It is plausible then that the decline in meeting attendance identified in Table 4.4 is, in part, due to perceptions of the declining effectiveness of such meetings. We will return to this issue below.

The third dimension of party activism is that of representation, and this is discussed next.

The representation dimension of activity

Representation refers to activities such as holding elective office, either within the party organization or on outside bodies such as the local council, a National Health Service trust, or the governing

Table 4.6 The representation dimension of activism (percentages)

	1990	1997	1999
Stood for office in party in last five years	30	17	19
Stood for office outside the party in the last five years	15	11	13
Currently hold office in party	14	11	13
Currently hold office on an outside body	15	N/A	N/A

body of a local school. This type of activity involves high-intensity participation, since the meetings of party committees or local council committees can take up a great deal of time, particularly if the party controls the local authority. Not surprisingly, the representation dimension of activism involves a much smaller proportion of the members than the other dimensions.

As can be seen in Table 4.6, in 1990 about 30 per cent of the Labour Party members surveyed had stood for office within the party organization on at least one occasion within the previous five years. By 1997 this figure had nearly halved, indicating a steep decline in the number of members standing for office within the party over this period. Interestingly enough, the numbers of people willing to run for office outside the party organization declined much less over the period, although some decline in this activity was also apparent. A further breakdown of the type of offices held within the party showed that about 70 per cent were at the branch level, the lowest level of organization, and the remaining 30 per cent were at the constituency level. These proportions did not change significantly over the nine-year period.

Party members who hold office within the organization at the constituency level or on an outside body are the really high-intensity participants and we should not expect a large proportion of members to be involved in these types of activities. But the changes in the competitiveness of elections for party offices over this period is a further symptom of a decline in activism within the grassroots party.

Another aspect of the party members' representative role is the extent to which they are involved in other types of organizations. This is an aspect of their role as 'ambassadors in the community'. Their role in outside voluntary organizations is not a formal one of representing the party, but rather an informal one of voicing the party point of view in the wider community. This is the organizational counterpart to the informal communications discussed in Table 4.3. The data in Table 4.7 illustrates the importance of this aspect of representation.

It is clear from Table 4.7 that a significant number of party members are involved in a wide range of educational, community, cultural and political organizations, but, unsurprisingly, a greater proportion of them are members as distinct from being volunteers who do unpaid work for the organization. There are no clear trends over the two-year period in membership or voluntary activity in these organizations, except in relation to the membership of trade unions and professional organizations. The level of membership of both of these types of organization grew among grassroots Labour Party Members. It seems plausible that the arrival of a Labour government changed the climate in which these organizations operated and this in turn stimulated party members to join trade unions and professional organizations in greater numbers. At a time when the leadership of the party has distanced itself from the trade union movement, one might have expected to see a decline in trade union membership at the grassroots. In fact, rather the opposite has happened and party members remain attached to trade unionism in large numbers.

Overall, representation is a key activity if the party organization itself, not to mention outside bodies in both the voluntary and state sectors, are to function effectively. This takes us to the fourth and final aspect of party activity: donating money to the organization.

Donating money and party activity

Donating money to the party organization has already been touched on in relation to campaigning in Tables 4.4 and 4.5. But it is important to probe in a little more detail this activity, since this is a key function of party members from the point of view of the leadership. State funding of political parties is very limited in Britain. Moreover, the proposals of the Neill Committee (TSO, 1998) on the funding of political parties make it unlikely that state funding will increase to any significant extent in the future. This means that the dependence of parties on their members for funds is likely to increase, making the question of members' attitudes toward party donations an important one.

Table 4.7 Representation of members on outside bodies (percentages)

Type of organization	1997		1999	
	Belongs to	Does unpaid work for	Belongs to	Does unpaid work for
A group that helps the elderly, handicapped or disadvantaged people	15	9	12	9
Religious or church organization	12	3	13	6
Education, music or cultural group	17	4	17	8
Trade union	34	2	42	5
Local community action group	7	3	5	5
Third World or human rights group	13	2	10	3
Conservation or environmental group	15	1	11	2
Professional association	19	1	22	2
Youth group	4	3	2	2
Sports or recreation group	13	2	11	3
Women's group	4	1	5	2
Peace movement group	6	1	5	1
Animal rights group	5	1	3	1
Health-related group	5	2	4	4
Other type of group	9	3	7	5

Table 4.8 contains information about the total financial contributions made to the party over the period 1992 to 1999.[1] The data has been adjusted to reflect 1999 prices, making it possible to see how the donations made by party members have evolved over time. The most illuminating figure is the median contribution, since, unlike the mean, the median is not distorted by a few large donations.[2] This makes it the best measure for judging the amount of money given to the party by the average member. It can be seen that this median amount dropped from £42 in 1992 to £28 in 1999. In other words in 1999 the average member gave about two-thirds of the amount he or she gave to the party in 1992.

The standard deviations are a measure of the average dispersion of the distribution of donations, or the extent to which giving money to the party can vary around the average. It has grown considerably over time, particularly between 1992 and 1997. This means that a greater proportion of the members gave either less or more than the typical amount in the late 1990s compared with the early 1990s. In part this was a product of the fact that the percentage of members who gave less than £20 more than doubled between 1992 and 1999.

The data in Table 4.8 make the point that the willingness of party members to give money to the party organization declined over this

Table 4.8 Total amounts donated to the Labour Party by members

'What is your estimate of the total financial contribution which you made to the party in the last 12 months (including annual membership fee, contributions to local or national fund-raising initiatives, standing orders etc)?

	Percentages		
Value	1992	1997	1999
Up to £20	20	40	45
£21 up to £40	26	23	16
£41 up to £60	17	13	13
£61 up to £80	13	6	5
£81 up to £100	5	2	8
£100 plus	20	16	14
Mean	£77	£62	£78
Median	£42	£25	£28
Standard deviation	£166	£316	£246

Note: Expressed in 1999 prices.

ten-year period. In that respect giving money is rather like the contact, campaigning and representation dimensions of party activism, all of which have also declined to varying degrees during this period. There is no evidence to suggest that members might be more willing to give money to compensate for their declining activities in other directions. Rather than being a substitute for other types of political activity, donating money appears to be a complement to those activities.

Table 4.9 provides three overall measures of activism which combine together the different types of activities discussed up to this point. They provide summary measures of the state of activism in the grassroots Labour Party over this ten-year period. It can be seen that there has been a significant growth in the proportion of members who do no work at all for the party in the average month. This group grew from around half of the members in 1990 to nearly two-thirds by the end of the decade. A less dramatic decline took place in the proportion of members who are very active, defined as the proportion working more than ten hours for the party in the average month. This figure fell from 10 per cent in 1990 to 6 per cent in 1997.

Table 4.9 Summary measures of activity in the grassroots party (percentages)

'How much time do you devote to party activities in the average month?'			
	1990	1997	1999
None	51	63	65
Up to 5 hours	30	25	22
From 5 up to 10 hours	10	6	7
From 10 up to 20 hours	6	3	3
More than 20 hours	4	3	4
'How active do you consider yourself to be in the Labour Party?'			
Not at all active	—	31	40
Not very active	—	42	35
Fairly active	—	19	17
Very active	—	8	8
'Are you more active or less active within the party than you were five years ago (or when you joined if less than five years ago), or about the same?'			
Less active	43	29	48
About the same	38	53	43
More active	20	18	9

A similar pattern exists in the subjective measures or self-reported levels of activism in Table 4.9, although in the case of the second sub-table there is no data available from the earlier period. However, the evidence suggests that the proportion of members who consider themselves to be not at all active increased in the period between the general election of 1997 and the mid-term in 1999. The most striking evidence relates to the third sub-table, in which members were asked about changes in their perceived levels of activism over time. In this ten-year period the proportion of members who thought that they were less active always outnumbered the proportion who thought that they were more active. But the ratio of less active to more active changed dramatically, from about two to one in 1990 to nearly five to one in 1999.

Overall, the evidence suggests that there has been a significant decline in all types of party activism in Labour's grassroots during this period. In the next section we examine why this has occurred.

Explaining the decline in activism

In order to explain the decline in activism which has occurred over time in the Labour grassroots party, it is necessary to have a theoretical explanation of why people become active in the party in the first place. Once participation is explained it becomes possible to understand why it has declined. This can be done by using the general incentives theory which was developed in order to explain why people join parties in the first place and why some of these recruits become active once they have joined (Seyd and Whiteley, 1992; Whiteley, Seyd and Richardson, 1994; Whiteley and Seyd, 2000). We briefly explain this model, before examining evidence relating to it as an explanation of activism in the grassroots Labour Party.

The general incentives model

The general incentives model of participation was introduced specifically to explain high-intensity types of participation such as canvassing, attending meetings and running for office, which are the focus of our concerns in this chapter (see Seyd and Whiteley, 1992; Whiteley, Seyd and Richardson, 1994; Whiteley, Seyd, Richardson and Bissell, 1994; Whiteley and Seyd, 1998a). The theory is really a synthesis of rational choice and social-psychological accounts of participation. The former theories stress the role of calculations of costs and benefits in the decision to participate and the latter the role of social norms and internalized values.

The essence of the general incentives theory is that actors need incentives if they are to participate in politics. These incentives are fairly wide ranging and are broader than narrowly-defined individual incentives of the type which typically appear in rational choice models (see Olson 1965; Green and Shapiro, 1994). The theory proposes that five types of incentives explain participation; these are collective, selective, group, and expressive incentives, and, finally, incentives derived from social norms. In addition, the theory suggests that perceptions of the costs of activism and the individual's sense of political efficacy need to be taken into account in order to explain participation.

To briefly discuss each of the incentive measures in turn, collective incentives are those derived from policy goals, that is individuals participate in politics in order to promote particular policies that they favour, whether it be increasing pensions, banning the bomb, spending more money on the health service or bringing back the death penalty. This might seem a self-evident motive for participating in politics, but it does raise a difficult logical problem.

Policy goals of the type we have mentioned are 'collective goods' (see Olson, 1965), that is once they are provided they are available to everyone, not just to the individuals who campaigned for their provision in the first place. Thus if party activists work to promote higher pensions and are successful, then the benefits will go to all retired people and not just to the retired (or other) party members who campaigned for them. Indeed the benefits will go to political opponents as well as to political supporters. For this reason, individuals have an incentive to 'free-ride' on the efforts of others – to let others do the work of campaigning for such benefits and then to enjoy them if such campaigns are successful. This makes a notion of party activism motivated solely by collective incentives problematic.

In the standard specification of the model collective incentives are weighted by the individual's sense of political efficacy. The latter refers to the extent to which individuals feel that they can change things and have an influence on outcomes in politics. Clearly, before they translate a desire to promote policy goals into activism, they have to feel that they can make a difference to outcomes and this is what political efficacy means. An alternative specification of the model sees efficacy as operating independently of policy goals, but nonetheless having an important influence on activism. Either way, it is important to take into account the extent to which people feel a sense of efficacy when they are deciding to participate in politics.

As well as considering collective benefits from political action it is also important to examine the costs of such action. Individuals may be aware that participation takes up time and effort and this can deter them from being involved. This would particularly be true of individuals who are raising a family or who work long hours. So an important consideration in understanding why some people are involved in politics when others are not, is differences in the perceptions of the costs of such activities in the minds of party members.

Selective incentives are different from collective incentives in that they refer to the benefits of political activity received by people who get involved which are not received by non-participants. This means that they are not subject to the 'free-rider' problem associated with collective incentives. There are three types of selective incentives: process, ideological and outcome. Process incentives refer to motives for participating which derive from the process of participation itself and have two aspects; one is related to enjoying politics for its own sake and the other depends on interacting with like-minded people within the party organization. For some people, the political process is interesting and stimulating in itself, regardless of the outcomes or goals. Participation is a way of meeting like-minded people, and for some this is motive enough for getting involved.

A second type of selective incentive is ideology, which is another type of process incentive. Ideological radicalism should motivate some individuals to join the Labour Party because it allows them to interact with like-minded people and give expression to deeply held beliefs. Their involvement is prompted by similar motives as the active churchgoer: membership of the church allows religious people to give expression to their beliefs, as well as to become part of the congregation.

Selective outcome incentives refer to motives concerned with achieving personal advancement in politics. Some party activists harbour ambitions to become a local councillor, for example, or the local mayor, or even to be elected to the House of Commons. Others may want nomination from their party to become a school governor, or a local magistrate. Since elected representatives have to serve an 'apprenticeship' within their party organization before they are chosen for elective office, activism can be regarded as an investment which must be made if the individual has ambitions to develop a future career in politics.

Group incentives for participation depend upon individuals thinking about the efficacy of the group as a whole. The suggestion is that one reason why some individuals participate is because they believe that their party makes a difference to society. If they believe this, then they will join and may become active. This is an aspect of 'civic culture' in which parties are seen as key institutions in changing society (see Almond and Verba, 1963: 105; Muller and Opp, 1986, 1987). Members participate because they feel part of a successful organization which they think is able to change Britain.

Such group incentives for participation are not compatible with a narrowly-defined rational actor model of participation, in which individuals count the costs and benefits of collective action for themselves acting alone. Individuals acting alone are not in a position to influence the political effectiveness of a national organization such as a political party, since their contribution to this effectiveness is so small. Moreover, they can 'free-ride' on the efforts of others. For these reasons, it is not rational for them to evaluate their own participation in relation to the performance of the group as a whole (see Whiteley, 1995). However, from a social-psychological perspective, the group solidarity engendered by success does provide an incentive to participate, independently of other factors.

Another set of factors which explain participation within the general incentives framework are motives based on expressive or affective attachments to a party. These motives also lie outside the standard cost–benefit model of decision-making, with its emphasis on cognitive calculations, and are rooted very much in the social-psychological research tradition. Such motives have long been discussed in the literature on party identification, since the early theorists (see, for example, Campbell et al., 1960) saw partisanship as an affective orientation towards a significant social or political group in the individual's environment.

Accordingly, we reason that some people will be motivated to join and be active by an expressive attachment to their party, which has little to do with the benefits they might receive from membership, either at the individual or collective levels. Such motives for joining are grounded in a sense of loyalty and affection for the party, which is unrelated to cognitive calculations of the costs and benefits of membership.

The final motive for activism in the general incentives model derives from social norms. This refers to the influence of other people on the individual's willingness to participate. One interpretation of this, which derives from the civic voluntarism model of participation (see Verba, Schlozman and Brady, 1995), suggests that individuals participate more if they are asked to do so by a 'significant other' such as a spouse or a parent. This is referred to as political mobilization. In other words when they are recruited into the party by someone who is close to them, they are likely to take membership more seriously and to get more involved than if they were recruited by a stranger or by an impersonal mechanism such as a newspaper advertisement. In this sense social norms have an influence on activism.

Overall, then, the general incentives theory of political participation postulates that a number of distinct factors are at work in explaining why people join a political party, or become active once they have joined. Some of these factors are grounded in rational choice theory, but the theory goes beyond a narrow rational choice conception of participation to examine broader motives for involvement, derived from social-psychological theories. In the next section we examine evidence in support of this theory of participation.

The evidence for the general incentives theory

The relationship between collective incentives and activism in 1997 is shown in Table 4.10. Each of the indicators in this table relate to policies which played a prominent role in Labour's election campaign just prior to the survey. Thus the manifesto spoke about the need to 'save the NHS' (Labour Party, 1997a: 20); the need to 'stop the growth of an underclass in Britain' (Labour Party, 1997a: 19); to 'help parents balance work and family' by giving workers new rights (Labour Party, 1997a: 25); and in general the manifesto called for greater spending on education, health and social welfare, albeit coupled with a promise not to increase the basic rate of tax.

Table 4.10 Relationships between collective incentives and members' activism in 1997 (percentages)

Collective incentives	Not at all active	Not very active	Fairly active	Very active
The government should spend more money to get rid of poverty				
Definitely should	55	59	65	72
Probably should	38	36	31	24
Doesn't matter	3	2	2	2
Probably should not	4	3	1	2
Definitely should not	1	0	1	1
The government should put more money into the National Health Service				
Definitely should	73	74	78	82
Probably should	25	24	20	16
Doesn't matter	1	1	1	1
Probably should not	1	1	1	1
Definitely should not	0	0	0	1
The government should give workers more say in the workplace				
Definitely should	41	45	54	60
Probably should	48	45	40	34
Doesn't matter	7	7	4	3
Probably should not	4	2	2	2
Definitely should not	1	1	1	1

Table 4.10 (continued)

Collective incentives	Not at all active	Not very active	Fairly active	Very active
The government should reduce spending generally				
Definitely should	5	4	5	6
Probably should	27	26	24	19
Doesn't matter	11	10	9	9
Probably should not	36	38	37	39
Definitely should not	21	22	25	27

If collective benefits or policy promises by the party promote activism, then we would expect to see activists supporting spending on the health service and on poverty in greater numbers than the inactive. Similarly, the activists should be more enthusiastic about workers' rights and be less supportive of general spending cuts than the inactive. As Table 4.10 shows, all these predictions are supported by the evidence. Thus 72 per cent of members who define themselves as very active think that the government should spend more money to get rid of poverty, compared with only 55 per cent of the inactive; 82 per cent of the very active support more money for the health service compared with 73 per cent of the inactive; 60 per cent of the very active support the idea of giving workers more say compared with 41 per cent of the inactive; and finally 66 per cent of the very active oppose cuts in public spending, compared with 57 per cent of the inactive. Clearly the evidence suggests that support for the party's collective goals is associated with being active.

In the case of selective incentives, relationships between activism and the attitude indicators are even stronger than for collective incentives. The first two indicators in Table 4.11 relate to outcome incentives, or the desire of the respondent to develop a career in politics. It is important to note that this is measured indirectly in the survey, by asking respondents to comment on statements, rather than asking them outright if they want to become a local councillor or an MP. This was done because pilot work in the early stages of the survey design showed that party members were rather reluctant to admit to having political ambitions. A social norm exists within the Labour Party which inhibits members from expressing a desire to become politicians.

Notwithstanding the last point, it is clear from Table 4.11 that activists were much more likely to say than inactive members that people like themselves could do a good job as an elected representative on the local council or in Parliament. The proportion of the very active who strongly agree that they could do a good job on the local council outnumbers the inactive who say this by a factor of nearly five to one. Similarly, four times as many very active members harbour strong ambitions to enter Parliament compared with inactive members.

The second two indicators in Table 4.11 relate to process incentives, or the desire to be involved in politics for its own sake. Once again we

Table 4.11 The relationship between selective incentives and members' activism in 1997 (percentages)

Selective incentives	Not at all active	Not very active	Fairly active	Very active
A person like me could do a good job of being a local Labour councillor				
Strongly agree	9	11	20	43
Agree	32	37	44	41
Neither	22	24	18	9
Disagree	28	23	15	4
Strongly disagree	9	5	3	3
Labour would be more successful if more people like me were elected to Parliament				
Strongly agree	5	6	8	20
Agree	16	21	28	26
Neither	38	40	37	32
Disagree	33	27	24	18
Strongly disagree	8	5	4	4

Table 4.11 (Continued)

Selective incentives	Not at all active	Not very active	Fairly active	Very active
Being an active party member is a good way to meet interesting people				
Strongly agree	5	7	12	22
Agree	46	55	63	62
Neither	36	29	17	12
Disagree	11	8	6	4
Strongly disagree	3	2	1	1
The only way to be educated about politics is to be a party activist				
Strongly agree	5	5	7	14
Agree	29	28	37	39
Neither	13	14	13	12
Disagree	43	46	38	30
Strongly disagree	10	8	5	6

observe significant differences between active and inactive members, with very many more of the former agreeing with the proposition that participating in politics is a way of meeting interesting people, than is true of the latter. A similar point can be made about the desire to get involved in order to be educated about politics.

This pattern of differences between active and inactive members continues in relation to the indicators of the costs of participation and group efficacy set out in Table 4.12. However, in the case of perceptions of costs, one of the measures does not work in the way that would be anticipated. According to the general incentives theory, perceptions that politics involves a lot of time and effort should deter people from participating, so that we would expect the active to discount such perceptions in comparison with the inactive. In other words, the inactive should be more in agreement with the statement that participation is bad for family life, since that perception is inhibiting their activism.

In the event, the evidence in relation to the first indicator in Table 4.12 is ambiguous. Some 82 per cent of the very active agree or strongly agree with this statement, compared with 76 per cent of the inactive, so in that respect responses are not as anticipated. However, it is also true that 9 per cent of the very active strongly disagree or disagree with the statement, compared with only 3 per cent of the inactive, which is consistent with expectations. Clearly the very active are more polarized on this measure than the inactive, making the relationship between activism and the measure inconclusive.

The second measure of costs relates to perceptions that attending meetings can be tiring after a hard day's work. In this case 24 per cent of the very active disagree or strongly disagree with the statement, compared with only 7 per cent of the inactive. This second measure of perceptions of costs is clearly consistent with theoretical expectations.

The group efficacy measures are indicators of the extent to which members feel that they are part of an effective organization which can change Britain. It is clear that the very active are more likely to feel this than the inactive. Thus 52 per cent of the very active strongly agree that Labour Party members can change Britain, compared with only 28 per cent of the inactive. Once again, perceptions of group efficacy are associated with participation in the grassroots party.

Table 4.12 The relationship between members' perceptions of the costs of participation, group efficacy and activism in 1997 (percentages)

Perceptions of costs and group efficacy	Not at all active	Not very active	Fairly active	Very active
Party activity often takes time away from one's family				
Strongly agree	13	11	13	25
Agree	63	62	62	57
Neither	21	21	16	9
Disagree	3	5	9	8
Strongly disagree	0	0	1	1
Attending party meetings can be tiring after a hard day's work				
Strongly agree	15	12	10	13
Agree	56	60	60	55
Neither	22	18	12	8
Disagree	7	9	17	21
Strongly disagree	0	1	1	3

Table 4.12 (Continued)

Perceptions of costs and group efficacy	Not at all active	Not very active	Fairly active	Very active
When Labour Party members are united they can really change Britain				
Strongly agree	28	32	40	52
Agree	58	58	54	42
Neither	11	8	5	4
Disagree	3	2	1	1
Strongly disagree	1	0	0	0
Labour Party members are part of a great movement of like-minded people				
Strongly agree	6	7	11	14
Agree	38	42	46	45
Neither	27	26	22	19
Disagree	26	22	19	19
Strongly disagree	3	3	2	3

Similarly, the very active are twice as likely as the inactive to agree strongly that they are part of a great movement.

Table 4.13 contains indicators of expressive incentives and social norms as predictors of participation. In the case of expressive incentives, there is a powerful relationship between activism and the strength of the attachment to the Labour Party. Some 88 per cent of the very active were very strongly attached to the party, compared with only 38 per cent of the inactive. Clearly, expressive attachments play an important role in explaining why some people become active in the party.

The second sub-table in Table 4.13 examines the relationship between social norms and activism, measured in terms of the recruitment of members to the party. It will be recalled that the basic idea here is that individuals who are recruited to the party by 'significant others', or people who they know and trust, are more likely to become active than people recruited by impersonal mechanisms such as a national party advertisement or an individual who they do not know personally. The first four rows of the sub-table refer to the impersonal mechanisms of recruitment and the last four to face-to-face and personal mechanisms.

The table shows that there is a clear tendency for members who were recruited by people they know to be more active than members who were recruited by impersonal means. About 25 per cent of the inactive were recruited by impersonal means, such as a party political broadcast, a national party advertisement or a stranger who canvassed them, and 14 per cent of the very active were recruited in this way. In contrast 45 per cent of the inactive were recruited by friends, family or workmates, compared with 62 per cent of the very active who were recruited in this way. Thus it appears that recruitment into the party by someone who the individual knows personally has a significant influence on the likelihood that they will subsequently become active.

Finally, Table 4.14 examines the relationship between activism and indicators of political efficacy, which are also important in the general incentives theory. The evidence in the table shows that there is a clear relationship between activism and efficacy. Thus only 10 per cent of the inactive strongly agree with the statement that 'people like me have a real influence on politics', compared with 32 per cent of the very active. Similarly, 36 per cent of the inactive strongly agree

Table 4.13 The relationship between expressive incentives, social norms and activism in 1997 (percentages)

Expres[s]ive incentives, social norms and Party activism	Not at all active	Not very active	Fairly active	Very active
Strength of attachment to the Labour Party				
Very strong	38	43	64	88
Fairly strong	48	51	33	11
Not very strong	11	5	2	1
Not at all strong	3	1	0	0
Thinking about the circumstances when you actually joined the party. What triggered your decision to join?				
Telephone or door-to-door canvasser	3	3	4	5
Party political broadcast	7	5	4	2
National party advertisement	13	11	6	4
Local party newsletter	2	3	4	3
Trade union contacts	13	15	16	17
Work contacts	4	4	5	6
Family contacts	16	18	19	18
Social contacts	12	16	17	21

Table 4.14 The relationship between political efficacy and activism in 1997 (percentages)

Political efficacy	Not at all active	Not very active	Fairly active	Very active
People like me can have a real influence on politics if they are prepared to get involved				
Strongly agree	10	12	17	32
Agree	53	60	62	55
Neither	18	14	10	6
Disagree	17	13	10	7
Strongly disagree	3	2	1	1
Sometimes politics seems so complicated it is difficult for a person like me to understand what is going on				
Strongly agree	4	4	4	6
Agree	32	29	27	20
Neither	11	11	10	9
Disagree	38	43	42	42
Strongly disagree	15	14	16	24
The people who are most active in the Labour Party are the ones who have most say in deciding party policy				
Strongly agree	10	10	10	16
Agree	56	55	51	45
Neither	19	17	14	11
Disagree	14	16	23	23
Strongly disagree	2	2	2	5

or agree with the statement that 'politics is too complicated for a person like me', compared with only 26 per cent of the very active. Finally, 66 per cent of the inactive agree or strongly agree that activists have the most say, compared with 71 per cent of the very active. Being active in the Labour Party is clearly associated with feelings that the individual party member can make a difference in politics.

Up to this point we have shown that the various factors in the general incentives model have an influence on the likelihood that a respondent will be an activist. Clearly, if these factors explain the decline of activism in the grassroots Labour party, then they must have changed over time, and we consider this issue next.

Changing incentives for activism

To assess if the incentive measures are driving the decline in activism it is necessary to examine them over time. This can be done over a ten-year period by comparing the responses to these measures in the first survey of Labour Party members conducted in 1990 (see Seyd and Whiteley, 1992), with the most recent survey conducted in 1999. This comparison is made in Table 4.15.

Table 4.15 contains the percentages of respondents in 1990 and again in 1999 who strongly agreed or agreed with the incentives measures appearing in Tables 4.10 to 4.14. The main finding of this table is that every single indicator of incentives, with one exception, has changed in a way which reduces the respondents' incentives to be active. Furthermore some of the changes in these incentives have been quite significant.

In relation to collective incentives modest reductions have taken place in three of the indicators over time, and a small increase has taken place in the fourth. All of these changes create disincentives to participate, as can be seen from the relationships between activism and the incentives measures set out in Table 4.10. Thus, for example, the desire to give workers more say in the workplace fell by 6 per cent over the ten-year period, and since attitudes to this indicator are positively related to activism, such a decline serves to inhibit it. Similarly, an increase in the number of party members who favour cuts in government spending has the same effect, since it is the activists who oppose cuts in spending.

Table 4.15 Changing incentives for activism in Labour's grassroots, 1990 to 1999

Percentages agreeing or strongly agreeing	1990	1999	Change
Collective incentives:			
Spend more money on alleviating poverty	99	95	−4
Spend more money on the NHS	99	97	−2
Give workers more say in the workplace	93	87	−6
Reduce government spending generally	21	23	2
Selective incentives:			
People like me do a good job as councillor	48	46	−2
More people like me should be MPs	35	29	−6
Being active is a good way to meet people	68	58	−10
Being active is necessary to be educated	44	37	−7
Perceptions of costs:			
Party activity takes time away from family	82	74	−8
Meetings can be tiring	72	69	−3
Group incentives:			
Party members united can change Britain	92	82	−10
Party members part of a great movement	41	37	−4
Expressive incentives:			
Very strong identifiers with the party	55	41	−14
Political efficacy:			
People like me can influence politics	74	64	−10
Politics seems too complicated	35	31	−4
Activists have most say	70	60	−10
*Social Norms:**			
Percent recruited by people they know	60	39	−21

*Refers to members recruited up to 1994 compared with members recruited after that year

Changes in the selective incentive measures also serve to inhibit activism, particularly the measures of process incentives. The desire to be active in order to meet interesting people declined by 10 per cent over the period, and since this is positively associated with activism in Table 4.11, this change serves to inhibit participation.

The exception to this pattern occurs in relation to perceptions of costs. It will be recalled that the first measure of costs in Table 4.12 had an ambiguous relationship to activism. The very active were polarized in their opinions, being both more likely to agree and to disagree with the idea that activism restricts family life than inactive members. Since this indicator declined by 8 per cent over the ten-year period, it is not clear what effect this will have on activism. Such a decline will both promote and inhibit activism at the same time if the data from Table 4.12 are to be believed. Thus we cannot be sure of the effects of this change. On the other hand, it is also true that perceptions that 'Meetings can be tiring after a hard day's work' declined over time. In Table 4.12 activists were less likely to agree with this statement than the inactive, so a decline in overall agreement should promote activism.

Group incentives have also declined in a way which inhibits participation. Perceptions that Labour Party members could change Britain declined by 10 per cent over the time period. In addition, the belief that Labour Party members were part of a great movement of like-minded people also declined. Once again, these developments will have inhibited activism since, as Table 4.12 shows, the activists are more likely to believe these things than the inactive.

The second largest decline in Table 4.15 relates to expressive incentives, which was a particularly strong predictor of activism in Table 4.13. Clearly, something has happened to the Labour Party in the years between Neil Kinnock's leadership in opposition and Tony Blair's leadership in power which has reduced party members' expressive attachments to the party. One intriguing feature of this change is that most of it took place between 1997 and 1999. The 1997 survey of party members showed that about 50 per cent of respondents were very strongly attached to the party just after the general election took place, a decline of 5 per cent over 1990. This measure subsequently declined by a further 9 per cent between 1997 and 1999, which means that fully two-thirds of the decline over the ten-year period occurred in the two years of Labour in office. In other words Labour in power demotivated the grassroots members to a considerable extent. It is interesting that these were the years when Labour maintained stringent Conservative spending targets and, as a consequence, few benefits from Labour in power were apparent to the grassroots members. This may help to explain this development.

A similar point can be made about the changes in political efficacy, which are among the largest changes in the table. Perhaps the key indicator of efficacy is the statement: 'People like me can have a real influence on politics if they are prepared to get involved'. The figure for this indicator declined by 10 per cent, and again 8 of these percentage points occurred during the period 1997 to 1999.

The largest change in Table 4.13 relates to social norms, but this is calculated on a different basis from the other measures, because there was no comparable question in the 1990 survey. As the earlier discussion of Table 4.13 indicates, the key mechanism at work in promoting activism in relation to social norms is the fact of being recruited by someone who the individual knows personally. Accordingly, the social norms measure in Table 4.15 uses data from the 1997 survey to compare individuals recruited before Tony Blair became leader in 1994, with individuals recruited after that date. As the discussion in early chapters indicates, this was a period of rapid recruitment of new party members, which ensured that the party was about 40 per cent larger by 1997 than it had been in 1994.

However, the evidence shows that, in comparison with their predecessors, many more of these newer recruits joined the party as a response to impersonal recruitment mechanisms. The drive to recruit new members after 1994 concentrated on direct mailings, party political broadcasts and canvassing. This was effective in boosting the numbers but it did serve to dilute activism, because, as Table 4.13 shows, activists were more likely to have been recruited by people they knew rather than by impersonal mechanisms.

Conclusions

A long-term decline in activism has taken place within the Labour Party in the 1990s. This has affected all aspects of activism, including maintaining contact with other party members, communicating with the wider public, attending meetings, electoral campaigning and running for office, both within the party organization and outside. We have explained this decline in activism in terms of the general incentives theory, which suggests that declining incentives to participate are responsible for the phenomenon. All the incentives measures in the theory, whether they relate to policy goals, private incentives, expressive attachments, group loyalties or social norms, have contributed to the decline.

Compared with 1990 members are currently less likely to feel that they influence politics, less likely to enjoy politics for its own sake, less likely to be politically ambitious, less likely to think of themselves as participants in a great social movement, and, above all, less likely to be strongly attached to the party. Part of the reason for these developments is that the party recruited a lot of new members after 1994 and these people were different from its earlier recruits in a number of key respects. But this is not the whole story, since it is apparent that a decline has taken place in the incentives for activism among long-standing party members as well as the relative newcomers. This evidence suggests that the activist base of Labour Party politics, and possibly British party politics as a whole,[3] are in decay, and in the long run this does not augur well for democracy.

We return to this issue in the concluding chapter, but for the moment we go on to examine the role of party members in electoral campaigning, one of their key functions in the political system.

5
Activism and Campaigning in the New Labour Party

Introduction

In the British general election of May 1997 the Labour Party won a landslide victory, winning no less than 64 per cent of the members of Parliament elected to the House of Commons. Labour's overall parliamentary majority of 179 was higher than ever before in its history and larger than the number of Conservative MPs elected. The party succeeded in winning two million more votes than in the previous general election of 1992 and its share of the vote increased by 9 per cent. This success was repeated in the 2001 general election, although this election was accompanied by a dramatic fall in the turnout.

If the 1997 and 2001 elections were triumphs for Labour, they were also successes for the Liberal Democrats. In 1997 the Liberal Democrat overall share of the vote fell by 1 per cent in comparison with the election of 1992, but the party nonetheless more than doubled their representation in the House of Commons, from 20 MPs in 1992 to 46, giving the party its largest representation in the House since 1929. They built on this success by winning just over 18 per cent of the vote in 2001 and 52 seats.

Explanations for the defeat of the Conservative government concentrate on its performance from 1992 onwards. Economic mismanagement, in particular the withdrawal from the European exchange rate mechanism (ERM) in September 1992, broken promises, especially on taxes and the public services, and a collapse of trust, fostered by bitter intra-party conflict and well-publicized financial irregularities by some Conservative MPs, are emphasized. In addition, Tony

Blair's election as Labour Party leader and his subsequent creation of New Labour is regarded as a contributory factor (Denver, 1997; Butler and Kavanagh, 1997; Clarke, Stewart and Whiteley, 1997; King, 1998).

Such explanations tend to suggest that the outcome was determined in the years prior to the election so that the six-week election campaign had little impact upon the outcome. King, a strong advocate of this view, writes that 'all the evidence suggests that the campaign was largely irrelevant' (1998: 179). He continues:

> The politicians, as they always do on these occasions, puffed, panted, and rushed about the country. They stretched every sinew and strained every nerve. They gave speeches, they gave interviews, they gave their all. No camera angle was neglected, no photo opportunity was missed. At times the politicians resembled those manic characters in the jerky, speeded-up film comedies of the 1920s. But nothing happened. The audience, for whose benefit all these entertainments were laid on, remained almost completely inert. Scarcely a cough or a sneeze could be heard from the pit. (1998: 179)

In a similar vein, Ivor Crewe (1997) writes: 'Had there been no campaign and no Millbank, Labour would have still won by a mile. The election was decided long before the campaign by events in the first half of the 1992 parliament.' When assessing the importance of election campaigns it is important to distinguish three features of the parties' attempts to win support. First, there are the national campaigns directed and run from party headquarters which include press conferences, leaders' speeches, party election broadcasts and advertising. Then there are national attempts to direct local campaigns by targeting specific marginal constituencies. Finally, there are the purely local campaigns mounted by the grassroots party members in the parliamentary constituencies across the length and breadth of the United Kingdom.

If the national campaign is regarded as being irrelevant by some students of electoral politics, then arguably this is even more true of the local campaigns. Certainly, the 'Nuffield' election studies have consistently argued this point (see, for example, Nicholas, 1951; Butler, 1952). In the Nuffield study of the 1992 general election, for example, Butler and Kavanagh wrote: 'It is hard to locate any evidence of great benefits being reaped by the increasingly sophisticated and computerised local campaigning' (1992: 245). In the 1997 Nuffield study, Curtice and Steed analysed the detailed general election results in an appendix, part of which focussed on the targeting of marginal constituencies in the campaign by the political parties. They concluded that:

> The 1997 election does not appear to support claims made that local campaigning can make a difference in respect of other parties performances too. The Labour party targeted 90, mostly marginal Conservative constituencies... Yet... the performance in these constituencies was very similar to that in other Conservative/Labour contests. (Butler and Kavanagh, 1997: 312)

Ivor Crewe (1997) took an even firmer view and claimed that neither the Conservatives' 'weak and ageing constituency associations' nor 'Millbank's ruthless concentration on Labour's 100 target marginals' had any impact on the election outcome.

There is, however, growing evidence which contradicts this view, and which suggests that local campaigning can influence both voting behaviour and turnout in general elections. Some of this research uses campaign spending as a surrogate measure of campaign activity (see Johnston and Pattie, 1995; Johnston, Pattie and Johnston, 1989; Pattie, Johnston and Fieldhouse, 1995; Whiteley, Seyd and Richardson, 1994). This is spending that the local parties are legally allowed to make on campaigning during the election, and, unlike national campaign spending, it is tightly regulated. Other research uses surveys of party members who do the campaigning, in order to assess effects (Seyd and Whiteley, 1992; Whiteley and Seyd, 1994, 1998b) and a third approach uses surveys of constituency agents from the main parties who run the local campaigns (Denver and Hands, 1985, 1997). All of these approaches show that local campaigns are important. The findings from this type of work are summarized by Denver and Hands in their study of campaigning in the 1992 general election. They conclude that:

> This study of constituency campaigning in the 1992 general election has shown very clearly, we would suggest, that the easy

generalisation made in many academic studies – that, in modern conditions, local campaigning is merely a ritual, a small and insignificant side show to the main event – is seriously misleading. (Denver and Hands, 1997: 305)

Clearly, there is a basic disagreement over this question, and the purpose of this chapter is to try to resolve this disagreement by examining the impact of local campaigning on the vote for the Labour Party in 1997. We examine evidence relating to the 2001 election in Chapter 7. This analysis will also try to explain why swings to Labour were no larger in the targeted marginal seats than they were in other types of seats. We begin with an examination of the specific features of the 1997 general election, some of which support and some of which contradict the idea that local campaigns were important. This leads into a section in which a model of campaign effects is specified, and this is tested in a subsequent section using campaign spending data and information from the party membership survey.

Debates about campaign effects in 1997

As is well known, a key function of political parties in democratic systems is that of mobilizing voters to turn out and vote. Until quite recently the evidence on the effects of local campaigning on the vote was restricted almost entirely to the United States. Most of the US research suggested that campaigns had a significant influence on turnout in state and Federal elections (Cutright and Rossi, 1958; Cutright, 1963; Kramer, 1970, Crotty, 1971: Herrnson, 1986; Frendreis, Gibson and Vertz, 1990), and also on the vote share (Katz and Eldersveld, 1961; Patterson and Calderia, 1984; Huckfeldt and Sprague, 1992). Although, to be fair some of the findings are controversial (see Pomper, Moakley and Forth, 1980; Gibson and Smith, 1984).

In addressing the British debate about the impact of local campaigns on the vote in 1997, there are arguments which oppose and arguments which support the view that local campaigns are important. To consider the case against first, an important point is that the general election was a landslide victory, producing an unprecedented swing from the Conservative to Labour of more than 10 per cent (Times Newspapers, 1997: 280). In this context it is possible that the local campaigns were simply swamped by the impact of national voting trends in what has been described by some researchers as a realigning election (Evans and Norris, 1998). In this view local campaigns might have had an influence at the margins, but they were essentially irrelevant in the context of an election which Labour dominated so completely. This kind of reasoning implies that local campaigns might only be really important in 'normal' elections.

A second argument is based on the point made by Curtice and Steed, discussed earlier, about the targeting of local campaigns. Clearly, to be most effective in influencing the outcome of a general election, local campaigning should be targeted on marginal or 'winnable' seats. The fact that, as Curtice and Steed point out, the swings to Labour were no greater in the Labour target seats than in other types of seats, suggests that local campaigns did not matter in 1997.

This issue is less of a problem for the Conservatives and the Liberal Democrats than for Labour. In the case of the Conservatives, Denver and Hands (1997: 257) showed that they were very inefficient at targeting seats in the 1992 election because of the independence of their local parties from Conservative Central Office. It appears that the Conservatives do their most effective campaigning in safe Conservative seats, rather than in the marginal seats which decide elections. Since it seems likely that this state of affairs continued in 1997, it implies that we will observe a weak or a non-existent relationship between Conservative campaigning and the marginality of the seat. In the case of the Liberal Democrats, Curtice and Steed concede that they 'were far more successful in those seats which they targeted than elsewhere' (1997: 311), so there is a clear relationship between Liberal Democrat local campaigning and electoral support.

Notwithstanding this last point, there is clearly a paradox which has to be explained in the case of Labour: Why was there little difference in the swings between the targeted and non-targeted constituencies? On the face of it this fact undermines the claim that targeted campaigning helps to win seats. We will return to this point below.

A third argument why local campaigns might well have been much less effective in 1997 derives from the evidence in the British Election Study surveys that campaign activities have been declining over time. In both the 1987 and 1997 British Election Study surveys, respondents were asked if they had been canvassed by one or more of the political parties during the campaign. In the 1987 survey some 47 per cent of respondents stated that a canvasser had called at their home during the campaign (BES, 1987). By the time of the 1997 election survey this figure had declined to 25 per cent of respondents (BES, 1997). Some of this decline might be explained by the switch to telephone canvassing from the more traditional door-to-door methods. However, since canvassing is one of the key methods of mobilizing the vote, this evidence suggests that campaigning may have weakened over time, which in turn would have reduced its impact on the vote.

There is a possible explanation for the evidence on the decline of canvassing. This is the decline of party activism in Britain, which was discussed in the previous chapter and applies to the Conservatives as well as Labour (see Whiteley and Seyd, 1998a). As we pointed out earlier, this decline is partly a matter of demographics – for example, the ageing of party members which has particularly affected the Conservatives – but it is also influenced by political events and changing incentives to participate. Since parties require a core of active members to organize and run local campaigns, then declining activism is likely to weaken those campaigns over time, which in turn reduces their impact on the vote.

Another factor which contributed to the decline in campaigning is the redistribution of constituency boundaries which occurred after the 1992 general election. Only 228 of the 659 constituencies in the United Kingdom were unaltered or minimally changed. This meant that local branches of the political parties had to undergo substantial reorganizations at the grassroots level, with many activists being moved from one constituency party to another. This process clearly had the potential to disrupt local party organizations and to weaken their capacity for campaigning during the general election.

The case for the impact of local campaigns on the vote contains several arguments. Firstly, there is the point that the strength of partisan attachments among voters, which have been weakening for decades, have now reached quite low levels in Britain. In the 1997 British Election Study, only 16 per cent of the electorate expressed on very strong identification with a political party, whereas 34 per cent had 'not very strong' attachments (BES, 1997). This contrasts with the 48 per cent having a strong attachment in 1964 (Heath et al., 1991: 13). In a panel study of the 1987 election campaign Miller concluded that: '(B)y the mid-eighties we have evidence that the British electorate was de-aligned and volatile. Its tendency to vote along class lines and, more directly important, its psychological attachment to parties was only half as strong as it had been twenty years earlier' (Miller et al., 1990: 11). Since the evidence suggests that these trends have continued, it is clearly much easier to influence voters by campaigns both at the national and local levels when partisan attachments have been weakened in this way.

A second and related point is that when electoral swings are fairly uniform across Britain, as they were in the 1950s and 1960s, there is little scope for local campaign effects. In their pioneering research on British electoral behaviour, Butler and Stokes calculated that the standard deviation of the two-party swing in the 1955 general election was 1.4 per cent, and in 1970 it was 2.1 per cent (Butler and Stokes, 1974: 121). However, by the 1990s this situation has changed, so that by 1997 the standard deviation of the two-party swing was 4.3 per cent, or more than twice as large (Butler and Kavanagh, 1997: 297). Clearly, there is much greater scope for local campaign effects when the changes in party support are so variable across the country.

A third factor suggesting that local campaigns might have been important in 1997 relates specifically to Labour. As we have pointed out earlier, the party succeeded in reversing the decades-long decline in individual membership by an active recruiting campaign after Blair became leader in 1994. Actually, as we pointed out in Chapter 4, many of these new members were not very active in their local parties, but nonetheless many of them took an active part in the 1997 general election campaign. In the case of Labour at least, the successful membership-recruitment strategy may well have offset the declining rates of activism referred to earlier in Chapter 4. If so, local campaigns would have been enhanced by the influx of new members.

Clearly, there are arguments both for and against the proposition that local campaigns played an important role in influencing the election result in 1997. In the next section we begin to examine the evidence relating to this debate from our survey of party members.

The evidence on local campaigns in 1997

The 1997 survey took place immediately after the general election and so campaigning activities were fresh in the minds of party members when they were filling in the questionnaires. Accordingly we probed for details of members' election-related activities dividing these into two broad types. Firstly, there were election-related activities which members may have done on several occasions during the campaign, such as canvassing or delivering leaflets. Secondly, there were activities which members would be expected to do only on one occasion, generally on polling day, such as helping to run a committee room and driving voters to the polling station.

Table 5.1 contains data on campaign activities running throughout the election period. It can be seen in this table that there was quite a lot of campaign activities going on during the general election. Some 20 per cent of members canvassed on two or more occasions and about the same proportion helped out at least once with a fund-raising event. Most impressive of all is that 40 per cent of the party members delivered leaflets on two or more occasions, which, given the size of the party at the time of the election, meant that about 160 000 people were involved in this important activity. At the same time some activities, such as telephone fund-raising, involved very few members and a similar point can be made about telephone canvassing.

Table 5.2 contains information on one-off activities, much of which took place on polling day, and it shows that just under half the party members were involved in at least one activity on the day of the election. Thus some 180 000 members were out on polling day

Table 5.1 Members' campaign activities during the 1997 general election (percentages)

'Again, thinking about the 1997 general election, did you:'

	Not at all	Once	Twice	Three or more
Telephone canvass voters on behalf of the party	90	2	2	5
Canvass door-to-door on behalf of the party	76	4	4	16
Help with party fund-raising events	80	8	5	8
Deliver party leaflets	52	8	9	31
Attend a party rally	78	13	4	6
Help organize a street stall	91	3	2	4
Help with party mailings	79	5	4	11
Help with telephone fund-raising	98	1	0	1

Table 5.2 One-off election-related campaigning by Labour Party members in the 1997 general election (percentages)

'Thinking about the 1997 General Election, we would like to ask you about your activities during the campaign. Did you:'

	Yes	No
Display an election poster	78	22
Donate money to party election funds	64	36
Help run a party election day committee room	17	83
Drive voters to the polling station	17	83
Take numbers at the polling station	26	74
Remind voters on polling day to vote	45	55
Attend the counting of votes	12	88

reminding Labour Party supporters to cast their vote. Equally, about 100 000 members were involved in taking numbers at a polling station.[1] Not surprisingly, fewer members were involved in the organizational tasks of running a committee room and attending the counting of votes. But overall the evidence suggests that many members were involved in election-day activities designed to get the vote out.

One of the interesting features of the 1997 general election campaign was that the party headquarters in Millbank concentrated as never before on the exercise of targeting marginal seats. It is interesting therefore to address the question of whether or not members campaigned in marginal constituencies other than their own, and the evidence relating to this issue appears in Table 5.3.

It can be seen that just under three in every ten members were asked to work in a constituency other than their own during the general election campaign. However, in the event only 9 per cent actually heeded the call and worked in a different constituency. Furthermore, if this 9 per cent is analyzed in terms of the amount of time spent campaigning, only about 3.5 per cent of the members spent most or all of their time in another constituency. In one sense this can be counted a success, since that percentage of the membership in 1997 represented about 14 000 people. But in another sense it was a failure, in view of the fact that only a small proportion of the individuals who were asked to campaign elsewhere actually did a significant amount of work in another constituency.

Table 5.3 Members' campaigning and electoral targeting in 1997 (percentages)

'During the Election campaign some party members were involved in campaigning work for a constituency party other than their own. How about you?

	Yes	No
Were you asked to work in another constituency?	28	72
Did you work for another constituency party?	9	91

'How much time did you spend working in another constituency?

Some of the time	4.3
Half of the time	1.4
Most of the time	1.9
All of the time	1.6

These data suggest a solution to the paradox referred to earlier, of the absence of a relationship between the target seats and the swing to Labour in 1997. The explanation is that, despite the great emphasis placed on targeting by the party headquarters in Millbank, the strategy was not implemented effectively. As we explained in an earlier paper: '(I)t appears that while many members were aware of the national strategy of targeting marginal constituencies, only a few of them actually heeded the call and campaigned outside their own areas, and the great majority of these only put in a token appearance' (Whiteley and Seyd, 1998b: 198). It is important to stress that the grassroots Labour Party did a lot of campaigning during the election, as the evidence in Tables 5.1 and 5.2 makes clear. However, such campaigning was not based on directives from party headquarters in Millbank.

Clearly, if Labour Party members campaigned extensively in many seats other than Labour's target seats, then they could have had an important influence on the vote which would not be identified by an examination of the target seats alone. This point is strengthened by the finding of Rossiter et al. (1999) that the increase in the Labour vote averaged 12.3 per cent in marginal and close constituencies where the party was placed second, compared with only 7.1 per cent in safe Labour seats (Rossiter et al., 1999: 158).[2] These 113 seats were a larger group of constituencies than the national target seats.[3] This evidence means that targeted campaigns made a difference, but the targeting was not in response to the directives from party headquarters. Rather it was organized by the members themselves at the grassroots level.

This suggests that nationally-directed and locally-directed campaigning are different things. In general, activists appear to make up their own minds about where to campaign, and they do so mostly in their own areas. There is a relationship between campaigning and marginality, as our survey evidence shows, but by and large this is because constituency parties in marginal seats are fairly active,[4] not because of an influx of Labour activists from other constituencies.

The experience of the Liberal Democrats reflects that of Labour. In the seats where the Liberal Democrats were in second place to the Conservatives, they increased their vote by 4.6 per cent, even though their overall vote share fell by 1.3 per cent in comparison with 1992 (Rossiter et al., 1999: 158). The difference is often explained in terms of tactical voting where the electorate backed the party most likely to defeat the Conservatives. However, it is important to remember that local party activists have an important role in making their electorates aware of the opportunities for tactical voting, and in that sense it is a product of local campaigns.

This strengthens the case that local campaigning had an important influence on the vote in 1997 and we examine this issue next.

Modelling the effects of campaigning on the vote in 1997

The survey of Labour Party members was conducted in 200 constituencies, randomly selected from all 641 constituencies in England, Wales and Scotland. It is possible to measure the amount of campaigning done by party members in each of these constituencies, and relate those measures to the Labour vote. The average number of respondents in each of the constituencies was just under 30, and so we can regard these constituency samples as separate surveys which can tell us the amount of campaigning going on at the local level during the election. Since the samples reflect the size of the parties in these constituencies they are a good guide to the total amount of campaigning carried out in these constituencies during the general election.

The index of campaign activities used to assess how active local parties were in the 1997 general election is constructed by adding together the activities of individual party members. To make it clear how this is done, we examine the case of a single constituency, Houghton and Washington East, which is a relatively safe Labour seat in Tyneside. This was chosen because it had an average number of party members in the sample – a total of 32 individuals. Table 5.4 contains information about the election-related campaign activities used to construct the scale in this constituency.

It can be seen in Table 5.4 that 25 of the members did no telephone canvassing at all during the campaign, and 3 of the members did this on three or more occasions. To calculate an overall campaigning score from Table 5.4, each individual appearing in the 'not at all' column scores 0 points; in the 'once' column 1 point; in the 'twice' column 2 points; and in the 'three or more' column 3 points. Thus the total score for the activity of telephone canvassing in the constituency was 9, that is three individuals times three points, reflecting the fact that all the active members appeared in the 'three or more' column. A similar calculation is carried out for each activity in the table, producing

Table 5.4 Number of members involved in campaign activities during the 1997 general election in Houghton and Washington East

'Again, thinking about the 1997 General Election, did you:'

	Not at all (0)	Once (1)	Twice (2)	Three or more (3)	**Total points**
Telephone canvass voters on behalf of the party	25	0	0	3	**9**
Canvass door-to-door on behalf of the party	19	0	0	8	**24**
Deliver party leaflets	17	2	1	8	**28**
Attend a party rally	19	3	0	4	**15**
Help organize a street stall	26	0	0	1	**3**
Help with party mailings	20	2	2	4	**18**
Help with telephone fund-raising	27	0	0	0	**0**
	Total Points = 97				

Note: Missing cases means that the number of respondents does not always equal 32.

24 points for canvassing door-to-door, and so on. At the foot of the table it can be seen that the party members from this constituency scored a total of 97 points for the 7 activities in the table.

The same exercise is repeated in Table 5.5, which examines the 'one-off' campaign activities undertaken by party members in the sample from Houghton and Washington East. These are the activities which appear in Table 5.3, and it can be seen that eight members helped to run an election day committee room, five drove voters to the polls, and so on. Altogether the overall total of points scored from this table was 78. If we combine this with the points scored from Table 5.4, then the Houghton and Washington East constituency obtained a total of 175 points on the election campaigning scale.

Clearly another constituency party could obtain a larger number of points than Houghton and Washington East for two reasons. One is that it had more members in the constituency sample who worked equally as hard as the members in Houghton and Washington East. A second reason is that it had the same number of members as this constituency, but these members worked harder in election-related campaigning than the members in Houghton and Washington East.

It is possible to calculate campaigning scores for each of the constituencies in our sample and then relate these scores to the Labour

Table 5.5 One-off election-related campaigning by Labour Party members during the 1997 general election in Houghton and Washington East (numbers of members)

'Thinking about the 1997 General Election, we would like to ask you about your activities during the campaign. Did you:'

	Yes	No	**Total points**
Display an election poster	27	5	**27**
Donate money to party election funds	16	12	**16**
Help run a party election day committee room	8	20	**8**
Drive voters to the polling station	5	21	**5**
Take numbers at the polling station	2	24	**2**
Remind voters on polling day to vote	15	14	**15**
Attend the count/celebration party	5	21	**5**
Total Points = 78			

vote in the 1997 general election. The implication of this being that constituency parties which do more work will have a bigger impact on the vote One complication, however, relates to the size of constituencies in Britain. They are quite variable, with the largest constituency in the sample containing more than 100 000 electors and the smallest just over 32 000 electors. A large constituency is likely to have more Labour Party members and on average to do more campaigning than a small constituency, but this is not necessarily going to have a bigger impact on the voters because the campaigning will be spread across more electors. In other words we really need a measure of the amount of campaigning per elector in a constituency.

This can be done by dividing the index of election activities by the number of electors in each constituency. For example, Houghton and Washington had an electorate of 67 343 at the time of the 1997 general election. Accordingly, we divide the index of election activities score of 175 by this figure, which gives a score of 0.0025986. Similar scores can be calculated for all the constituencies in our sample, allowing election-related campaigning per elector to be compared with the Labour vote in each case.

The relationship between the Labour vote share and the Labour campaign index for all 200 constituencies in the sample is shown in Figure 5.1. Each asterisk in the figure represents a different constituency and the upward sloping line shows the relationship which fits the scatter of constituencies most accurately with the smallest error.[5] The fact that the line slopes upwards to the right means that the Labour vote share increases as local campaigning per elector increases. The correlation coefficient, which appears below the figure, measures how closely voting and campaigning are associated.[6] If we interpret this correlation in terms of the effects of campaigning on the vote, it means that an increase in campaigning of 10 per cent is associated with an increase in the Labour vote of about 3 per cent. Clearly, this implies that campaigning by local parties can have a significant electoral payoff.

However, it would be premature to jump to conclusions about the magnitude of campaign effects using the information in Figure 5.1. This is because this figure only considers the relationship between the campaign index and the vote. However, when examining this relationship it is important to take into account other factors which might intervene to distort the picture. For example one such factor,

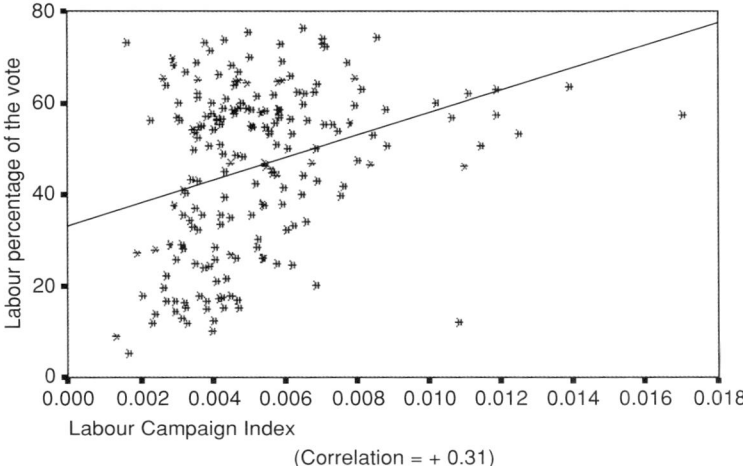

Figure 5.1 Labour vote and campaigning in the 1997 general election

which is not taken into account in the figure, is the social class characteristics of constituencies.

Although support for Labour was much less class-based than in the past (Kellner, 1997), it is nonetheless true that in the 1997 election Labour did well in constituencies with high concentrations of manual workers and less well in constituencies with many white-collar workers.[7] If a constituency has many manual workers then it is easier for the party to pick up votes compared with a very middle-class area, regardless of the amount of campaigning done at the local level, because the party has a bigger pool of sympathizers in that type of seat. For the same reason, Labour has more potential for recruiting members in working-class constituencies than it does in middle-class constituencies.

Consequently, the fact that campaigning appears to affect voting might be due entirely to the social class characteristics of constituencies rather than to the fact that voters are being persuaded to support the Labour Party by the activists. On the one hand, working-class people are more willing to vote Labour, regardless of the amount of campaigning done at the local level. On the other hand, more campaigning is being carried out in working-class seats, regardless of its effects on voting, because such seats may have more members. If social class explains both the higher Labour vote and the greater amount of campaigning, then the relationship between the two would be spurious and would not reflect a genuine causal link between campaigning and the vote.

There are other factors which can also distort this relationship. One is the amount of public sector housing or the number of council tenants in a constituency. Traditionally, the Labour vote has been higher among council tenants than among other working-class voters (Heath et al., 1991: 106–8). Thus it is possible that constituencies with a high percentage of council tenants will have both a large Labour vote and also a more active local Labour party. Again, an apparent relationship between the vote and the activities of the local party members may be due largely to a third factor, the number of council tenants in a given constituency. Of course, sales of public sector housing initiated by the Conservatives in the 1980s have considerably reduced the number of council tenants in Britain, so this factor may have declined in importance over time. But it is nonetheless important to take it into account.

A third factor which might explain the link between voting and campaigning is the number of unemployed people in a constituency. In the past the unemployed have been significantly more likely to support Labour than the Conservatives (Heath et al., 1991: 165–8). At the time of the 1997 general election some 63 per cent of Labour voters thought that unemployment was the most important problem facing the country (Gallup, 1997: 21). Thus the Labour Party would have had an electoral advantage in constituencies with high levels of unemployment because those out of a job, together with their friends and families, would seek to punish the Conservative government (see Miller et al., 1990: 250–5). Again, this needs to be taken into account if the relationship between voting and campaigning is not to be distorted.

Finally, a fourth factor is the age profile of the electorate in constituencies. In general young people are less willing to participate in politics than their older counterparts (Parry, Moyser and Day, 1992: 156–61; Denver and Hands, 1997). Part of the reason for this is that young people are not so strongly attached to political parties and they are less interested in the political process in general. However, in a landslide election it is possible that these factors were overcome to some extent by the winning party, giving Labour an advantage over the Conservatives in seats with many young voters. Accordingly, we need to take into account the percentage of youth in the electorate in any analysis.

Clearly we can extend this list of factors which need to be taken into account and include other social and demographic characteristics of constituencies. However, these factors change only rather slowly over time; for example, the class composition of constituencies will change as new people move in and others leave an area, but such changes will take many years to have an effect on voting behaviour. Such factors are unlikely to change significantly between the 1992 and 1997 general elections.

With this in mind, one way to eliminate these distortions is to examine the relationship between the change in the Labour vote between two general elections and campaigning, rather than between the share of the Labour vote in 1997 and campaigning. If changes in the demographic characteristics of constituencies such as their class characteristics are slow to take place, then they will be too small to influence the change in the vote in only four years. A similar point can be made about the change in the number of council tenants, unemployed voters, young voters and other demographic factors. Thus we can control for the effects of these variables when assessing the impact of campaigning on the vote by looking at the change in the vote over time.

Figure 5.2 compares the change in the Labour vote share in our sample of constituencies between the 1992 and 1997 general elections with the constituency campaign index. It can be seen that the line of best fit still slopes up to the right, implying that more campaigning translates into a bigger change in the vote, but that the relationship is weaker than it was in Figure 5.1. As we know, Labour won the 1997 election by a landslide whereas it lost the 1992 election, so that the Labour vote shares rose in the great majority of constituencies between the two elections. The evidence in Figure 5.2 implies that if a local Labour party increased its campaign activities by about 10 per cent between the two elections, it would have increased the change in the Labour vote by an extra 2 per cent. Clearly, campaigning made the difference between winning and losing in a lot of marginal seats.

An alternative way of looking at the relationship between campaigning and the vote is to use campaign spending as a surrogate

128 *Activism and Campaigning*

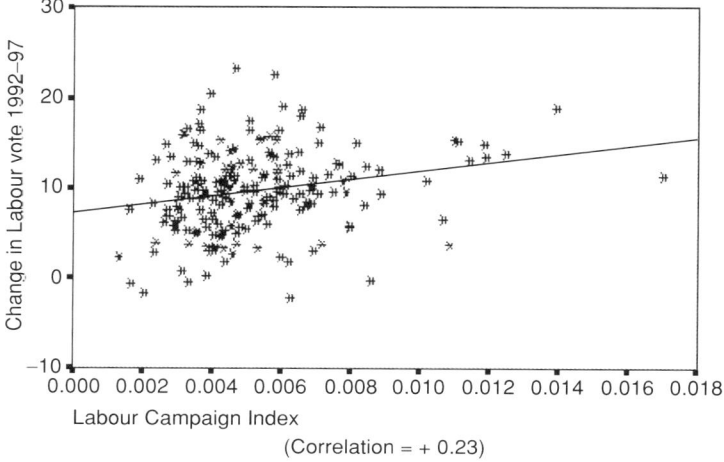

Figure 5.2 Change in the Labour vote 1992–1997 and campaigning

measure of election-related activity by local parties. As mentioned earlier, this has been used by a number of researchers as a proxy measure of campaigning in the past. On the legal definition, local spending includes the expenses of printing leaflets, advertising in local newspapers, telecommunications such as local phone canvassing, the cost of hiring rooms and holding public meetings, fees paid to agents and a variety of other things. Such spending is closely regulated by law with published maximum amounts allowed in different constituencies.

There, is of course, a relationship between the campaign index and the campaign spending variables, which is to be expected given that they are measuring different aspects of the same thing. This is demonstrated in Figure 5.3, where it can be seen that the correlation between the two measures is moderately strong. We have seen that the campaign index mainly measures 'labour' input, or the number of hours put in by individuals in campaigning. The spending scale mainly measures the 'capital' input, or the amount of money spent on advertising, publicity, administration and related activities rather than labour time. Clearly these two aspects of campaigning should work together to influence the outcome of an election at the local level.

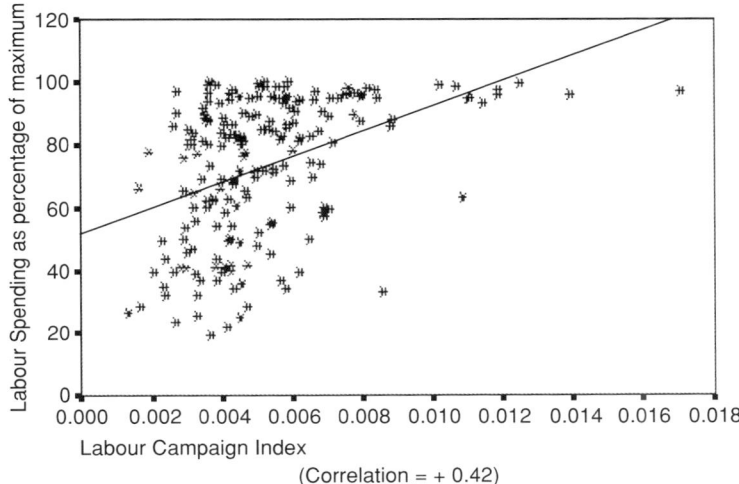

Figure 5.3 Labour spending as percentage of maximum and campaign Index

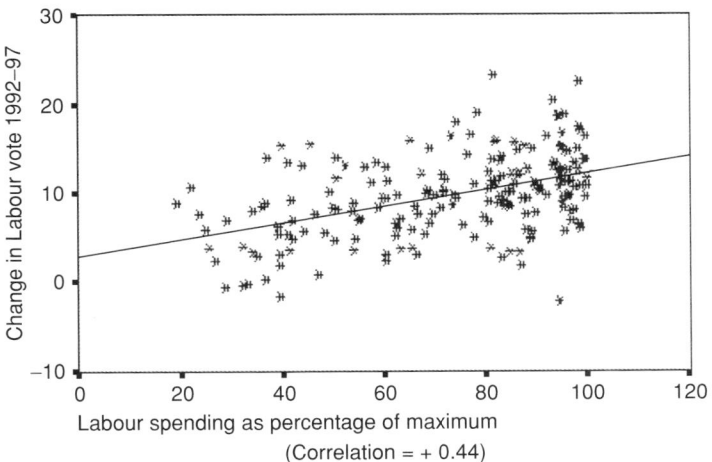

Figure 5.4 Change in the Labour vote 1992 to 1997 and campaign spending

The evidence in Figure 5.4 confirms that campaign spending has a positive impact on the change in the Labour vote between 1992 and

1997. In fact the correlation between spending and the change in the vote is rather stronger than the correlation between the campaign index and the change in the vote, observed in Figure 5.2. The correlation in Figure 5.4 suggests that a 10 per cent increase in campaign spending is associated with an increase of just over 4 per cent in the Labour vote. Clearly, both the 'labour' input and the 'capital' inputs into election campaigns make a difference to outcomes.

Up to this point we have considered only the relationship between Labour campaigning and the vote, but this is only part of the story. It seems plausible that if Labour campaigning and spending influences the Labour vote, then Conservative campaigning and spending will also influence it, but in the opposite direction. In other words the Labour vote share should be reduced by Conservative campaigning at the local level. Unfortunately there is no data available to construct a Conservative campaign index equivalent to the Labour measure. So we cannot reconstruct Figure 5.2 with a Conservative campaign index. But it is still possible to use the Conservative spending variable as a proxy measure for campaigning and to see how it relates to the Labour vote.

The relationship between the change in the Labour vote share and Conservative spending on local campaigning appears in Figure 5.5. It can be seen from this figure that surprisingly, there is a clear upward sloping relationship between the change in the Labour vote and Conservative campaigning. This means that the more work done by Conservatives at the local level, the larger the Labour vote. Thus Conservative campaigning appears to have the opposite effect to that which might be expected!

This apparently odd result can be explained by the finding of Denver and Hands (1997) that Conservative campaigning appears to be concentrated in safe Conservative areas, rather than in marginal seats or safe Labour seats. This largely comes about because local Conservative parties are strong in their safe seats but rather weak in marginal seats, and non-existent in safe Labour seats.

To see how this works, consider safe Labour seats to begin with. Here, neither Labour nor the Conservatives did any significant campaigning, so Conservative campaigning would have little effect on the change in the Labour vote. Next take the marginal seats, where both parties campaigned, but Labour campaigned more effectively. There the increase in the Labour vote will be greater, even though the

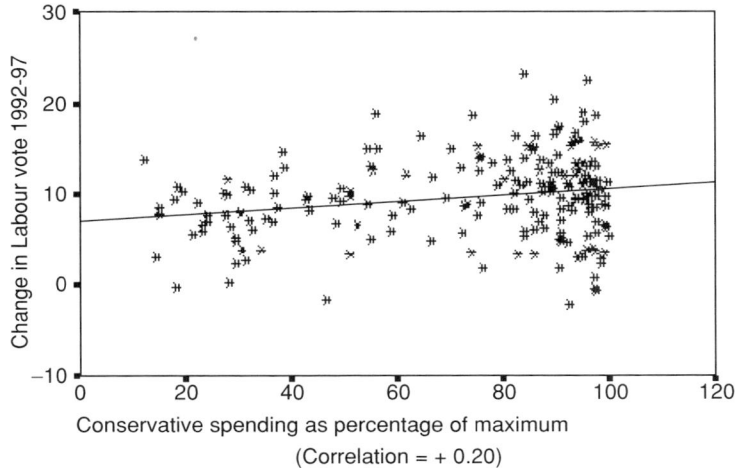

Figure 5.5 Change in the Labour vote 1992 to 1997 and Conservative campaign spending

Conservative are doing more work in comparison than their fellow party members in the Labour heartlands. Finally, consider safe Conservative seats, where Labour would have done little campaigning and the Conservatives quite a lot of campaigning. In this case such campaigning fails to influence the Labour vote very much because Labour support in those seats is quite small to begin with and cannot be changed much even by an intensive Conservative campaign.

The effect of all this would be to produce a perverse relationship between Conservative campaigning and the change in the Labour vote. Because of what happened in the marginals, the Conservatives will appear to be doing more work and getting a worse result. Overall, these patterns produce a positive relationship between Conservative campaigning and the change in the Labour vote, and the Conservatives will appear to do worse in constituencies where they do more campaigning. Clearly, this relationship would not exist if the Conservatives were able to distribute their campaign efforts more effectively.

As mentioned earlier, the Liberal Democrats were able to win more seats on a reduced share of the vote in 1997 compared with 1992, and this was because they were able to target their campaign efforts effectively. Figure 5.6 examines the relationship between the change

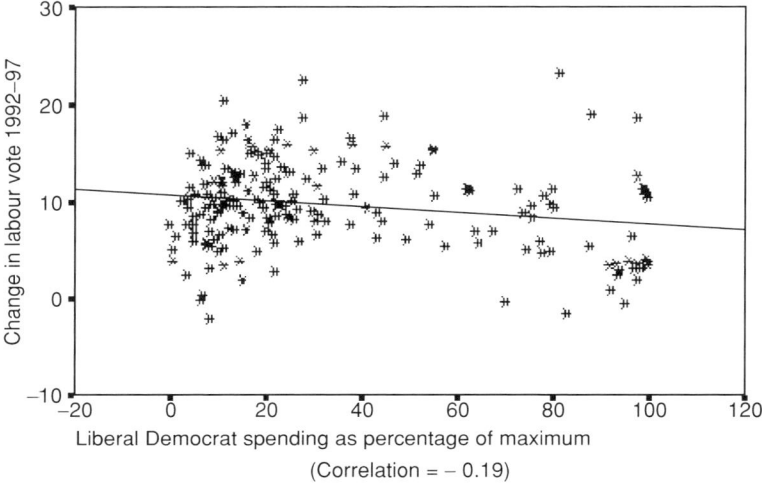

Figure 5.6 Change in the Labour vote 1992 to 1997 and LibDem campaign spending

in the Labour vote and Liberal Democrat spending on campaigns. It can be seen that there is a negative correlation between these variables, so that the Labour vote share declines as Liberal Democrat spending increases. In other words Labour was harmed by Liberal Democrat campaigning, which is exactly the result one would expect. The correlation suggests that a 10 per cent increase in the Liberal Democrat spending reduces the change in the Labour vote by about 2 per cent.

However, it is also true that the Liberal Democrats challenged Labour in only 11 seats in 1997, whereas they challenged the Conservatives in no less than 158. Thus the fact that Liberal Democrat campaigning reduced the Labour vote share did not mean that Labour lost many seats to them as a consequence. Rather the Liberal Democrat ability to target campaigns had the biggest effect on the Conservatives who lost seats to them in the election.

Up to this point the evidence suggests that campaigning had a significant influence on the Labour vote. But it is important to assess what these findings mean in terms of the number of seats which changed hands in response to the local campaign efforts in 1997. We examine this issue next.

Simulating the influence of campaigning on the seats won

It is, of course, possible that local campaigning had a significant influence on the vote while at the same time having a very small impact on the number of seats won by the parties. So it is important to assess the impact of campaigning on seats won or lost, and this will be the focus of the present section. To do this we need to take into account the campaigning done by all three parties, since, as we have observed earlier, Conservative and Liberal Democrat campaigning influences Labour's electoral support.

The model used to estimate the effects of campaigning on the Labour vote share is known as a multiple regression model, the details of which appear in the appendix to this chapter. The basic idea is that we predict the Labour vote share in 1997, using a number of different variables. Firstly, there is the Labour vote share in 1992, which controls for the effects of the demographic characteristics of constituencies of the type discussed earlier. The other variables are campaign measures relating to the three major parties.

The measures of campaigning include the campaign and spending indices for the Labour Party, campaign and spending indices for the Liberal Democrats,[8] and the spending index for the Conservatives. The model makes it possible to investigate the effects of campaigning by the three parties on the Labour vote share in our sample of 200 constituencies. The model is then used to predict the number of seats won by the parties in 1997, and since this model fits the data very well, it can be used to simulate the effects of the Labour campaign measures on the Labour vote.[9]

To examine the effects of campaigning on the vote, we set the campaign activities for the Liberal Democrats and the Conservatives at their actual levels in the 1997 election, while varying the rates of campaigning for Labour. The results of the simulations appear in Figure 5.7. They are re-scaled to show the effects of variations in campaigning on the entire Parliamentary Labour Party, rather than just on the 200 constituencies in the sample.

The column in the centre of Figure 5.7 indicates that the model predicts that Labour would win 411 seats when it campaigned at the actual levels achieved in 1997. Given that the party actually won 418 seats, the model is not completely accurate, but it is very close. The column immediately to the left of this middle column indicates that

134 Activism and Campaigning

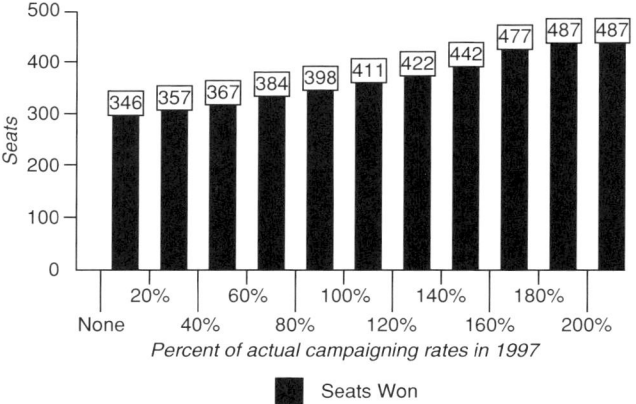

Figure 5.7 Simulations of Labour seats and campaigning

if the members had campaigned at a rate of 80 per cent of their actual campaigning, then the party would have won 398 seats.

Putting this another way a 20 per cent reduction in the actual campaigning carried out by members in 1997 would have cost the Labour Party 13 seats. Similarly, if the party had campaigned at 60 per cent of the 1997 rate it would have lost 27 seats, at 40 per cent 44 seats, and so on. If the party had done no local campaigning at all, then it would have lost 65 seats.

The simulation suggests that while the outcome of the general election was not determined by local campaigning, it is also clear that campaigning would have made the difference between winning and losing in a closer contest. For example, in the 1992 general election Labour won 271 seats and the Conservatives 336 seats, giving the latter an overall majority in the House of Commons of 22 seats. If the relationship between campaigning and the vote had been the same in 1992 as it was in 1997, then the simulations suggest that John Major would have lost his overall majority in that election if Labour Party members had campaigned some 20 per cent harder than they actually did campaign.

As we see in Figure 5.7, a 20 per cent increase in campaigning in 1997 would have won Labour an extra 11 seats, a 40 per cent increase an extra 31 seats, and so on. Again if the party members had campaigned at twice the rates they actually did, then the party would have won an extra 76 seats. In fact there appears to be no difference between campaigning at 180 per cent and 200 per cent of the 1997 rate, so campaigning meets diminishing returns beyond a certain point in terms of the number of seats won.

Discussion and conclusions

The results discussed in this chapter suggest that local campaigns played a very important role in influencing the vote in the 1997 general election. The campaign effects are measured by two different variables in the case of Labour and the Liberal Democrats and by one variable, campaign spending, in the case of the Conservatives. These findings reinforce our earlier conclusions from a survey-based analysis of Labour Party members (Seyd and Whiteley, 1992; Whiteley and Seyd, 1994), that local party activists play an important role in mobilizing the vote in British general elections.

The problem with arguments which reject these conclusions is that they are based on the extrapolation of trends in opinion polls or on an uncritical acceptance that targeting strategies by the national party organizations are a good guide to local campaign efforts, when they are not. It is clear that there is an important distinction to be made between nationally-directed constituency campaigns and locally-directed campaigns. The former are not particularly effective, while the latter are highly effective.

While it is true that Labour started the election campaign with a big lead over the Conservatives, the large changes in gross public support which can take place during the campaign indicates that opinion remains quite volatile and therefore malleable (see Miller et al., 1990). This is why campaigns, both local and national, can play a very important role in influencing the outcome. This evidence shows that the view that such campaigns are merely rituals undertaken by the parties with little or no relevance to outcomes is clearly wrong.

These results also have implications for academic debates about the nature of modern party organization. One dominant image is of the party as an 'electoral-professional' organization (see, for example, Panebianco, 1988) similar to that of a well-organized army. In this image the generals or party leaders manoeuvre the troops around the electoral battlefield and the latter willingly obey the commands of their superiors. This is clearly misleading, since in a real election the activists themselves tend to make judgements about where they will campaign independently of any national targeting strategy. This is not surprising since parties are largely voluntary organizations, not corporations nor armies, suggesting that the image of the electoral-professional party is misleading in key respects.

A similar point can be made about studies of campaigning which focus solely on the national level and ignore or discount the importance of local constituency campaigns (Gould, 1999). The magnitude of these local campaign effects suggests that parties which neglect and discourage their activists in the belief that they play only a ritualistic role in electioneering, are likely to pay a significant price in terms of seats lost in a general election. Indeed it is arguable that the decline in the Conservative grassroots party (see Whiteley, Seyd and Richardson, 1994) played an important part in explaining Labour's landslide win in 1997.

We began by examining arguments for and against the proposition that local campaigns matter in influencing the vote in a general election. Overall, these results indicate that the arguments against this proposition can be discounted. Local party activists play a much more significant role in influencing election outcomes, even in the case of a landslide election like that of 1997, than conventional wisdom allows.

Appendix: the Simulation Model

The Labour simulation regression model was as follows:

Lab97 = 11.02 + 453.75 Labour Index − 1367.49 LibDem index + 9.39 Labour Spending

$$(3.4) \qquad (4.6) \qquad (6.3)$$

−2.64 Conservative Spending − 2.98 LibDem Spending + 0.80 Lab92

$$(0.2) \qquad (4.6) \qquad (25.7)$$

| Adjusted R squared = 0.96 | F = 767.8 (t statistics in parenthesis) | N = 200 |

where:
Lab97 – the Labour percentage vote share in 1997
Lab92 – the Labour percentage vote share in 1992
Labour Index – the Labour campaign activities index

LibDem Index – the Liberal Democrat campaign activities index
Labour Spending – Labour spending as a percentage of the maximum
LibDem Spending – Liberal Democrat spending as a percentage of the maximum
Conservative Spending – Conservative spending as a percentage of the maximum.

It can be seen that all the variables in this model had statistically significant coefficients, other than the Conservative spending scale. The goodness of fit is very high, which is a prerequisite for a good simulation model.

6
What Do the Members Think of the Party and the Government?

Introduction

The aim of this chapter is to examine how the party modernization strategy, started by Kinnock in the 1980s and then continued by Smith and Blair, affected the attitudes of party members and voters over the ten-year period of the 1990s. The focus will be on their images of the Labour Party, as recorded from the time of our first survey in 1990 to the mid-term of the Labour government in 1999.

During the 1990s the Labour Party experienced radical changes both in relation to its internal structure, leadership and policies, and also in relation to its external electoral performance. In addition to revising policy positions, reshaping the internal party organization and changing its electoral strategy, the party sought to re-invent itself in the minds of the public. It is interesting to examine what the members thought about these changes. Did they regard them with enthusiasm or scepticism? And did they think that their own position had been strengthened or weakened by these developments?

The analysis in this chapter begins by examining the members' images of the party, or their beliefs about what the Labour Party stood for and who it sought to represent. An important component of this is the members' evaluations of the Labour leadership. In each case we examine the attitudes of members in 1990 and compare them with their attitudes in 1999, in order to get a full picture of how these changes have impacted upon grassroots' opinion over time. After examining members' attitudes to the party and the leadership, we then examine their attitudes at a more micro-level of analysis, by looking at their experience of participation in party meetings.

This is followed by a brief examination of trends in attitudes towards the same issues among Labour voters. In this case we use data from the 1987 and 1997 British Election Studies, a period which also spans a decade. So it is possible to get a picture of how both the members and Labour voters viewed the party over a ten-year period during which rapid changes took place.

After examining perceptions of the voters, we probe in more detail the background characteristics of the modernizers and traditionalists within the party, the former referring to members who supported the modernization strategy and the latter to members who were sceptical about it. The aim here is to examine what differences exist between these two groups.

In a fourth section we focus on the attitudes of members to their roles within the party organization. Some members expect to have a very active role in policy-making and so they are likely to be disillusioned by any leadership attempts to downgrade their role in the process of policy development. On the other hand there are members who attach little importance to their involvement in policy-making and who are content to let the leadership dominate this process. We examine the relative size of these groups and try to assess the extent to which members are likely to be alienated by the centralization of party structures which has taken place in recent years.

Finally, we examine members' attitudes to the performance of the Labour government, some two years after it took office. The 1999 survey provides the first opportunity to evaluate members' views on the performance of a Labour government during the ten years in which we have been conducting surveys of the grassroots party. These data give us the first clear insight into how Labour in power was seen by the members, and also to examine the implications of this for party strategy.

Members' images of the Labour Party, 1990 to 1999

What kind of party do the members consider the Labour Party to be? And in the light of their views on this question, is it possible to distinguish between those who accept the party reforms of recent years and those who are discontented about recent developments?

As we suggested earlier, Labour Party members are often discussed in contrary ways in the literature. Sometimes they are regarded as the reserve army of dedicated loyalists, who, though inclined to grumble, usually rally around their party and leader, giving him support and loyalty. At other times, they are seen as an 'awkward squad' who often embarrass the party and its leaders by making untimely and unappealing demands which undermine party unity.

The first interpretation draws on members' record of loyalty and deference to their leaders. Historically, such deference was due in part to a dominant trade union value system of unity and solidarity and, in part, to a working-class deference towards social superiors. Both these tendencies were aspects of what Drucker (1979) referred to as the ethos of the Labour Party. How much of this ethos has withered away in the contemporary Labour Party?

The second interpretation refers to numerous intra-party conflicts which have occurred over time and it suggests that members are assertive and questioning because they have distinctive political opinions which they want to express. Many are also natural rebels who inherently distrust authority since it is part of the 'establishment' that they are seeking to change.[1] This makes them aware of the corrupting nature of power, and they tend to distrust leaders who they are inclined to think will 'sell them out'. The spectre of Ramsay MacDonald, who abandoned the Labour Party while its leader in 1931, still haunts the party.

Are the members loyalists or rebels? There is evidence in the recent history of the Labour Party to sustain both interpretations. Now, however, we can examine the current attitudes of members and discover to what extent they are loyalists or an 'awkward squad', and in more general terms how they see the role of the party in contemporary British society.

There are three important aspects to members' perceptions of the party. Firstly, there are the general images of the role of the party in society. This aspect concerns the extent to which members think the party is united or divided, whether it is efficiently or badly run, and whether it has a middle-class or a working-class image. To evaluate this we have asked members to comment on descriptors of the Labour Party which provide an indication of how they feel about these generalized images.

A second aspect is the role of the party as an organization which represents various different interests in society. To examine members' perceptions of this we included a set of questions which asked members to assess the extent to which they thought that the party looks after different social groups, such as trade unions, business interests and ethnic minorities. Clearly, the first and second aspects are related, since if members feel that the party is looking after the interests of groups they care about, they are likely to have a favourable generalized image of the party.

A third important aspect of perceptions of the party is the evaluations of the leadership. Both Kinnock and Blair were modernisers, but the latter has a very different image from the former in the wider society. The very fact that Blair became Prime Minister whereas Kinnock remained in opposition creates a different context in which the members view the two leaders. It is interesting to assess how the images of the two leaders differ.

Leadership images refer not just to the party leader, but also to the other prominent senior figures who make up the Labour team at any point in time. A number of these individuals were prominent in party politics both in opposition in 1990 and in government in 1999. Accordingly, we probe what the members think of these prominent Labour parliamentarians who make up the collective leadership, and examine how attitudes to this group have changed over time. In passing we also examine their attitudes to the leaders of the main rival parties.

Table 6.1 Members' images of the Labour Party, 1990 to 1999 (percentages)

Please think about your general impressions of the Labour Party, and describe them using the following scales:

		Very	Fairly	Neither	Fairly	Very	
Extreme	1990	0	5	41	38	16	*Moderate*
	1999	2	8	35	35	20	
Efficiently run	1990	8	54	16	18	4	*Badly run*
	1999	17	52	14	13	3	
United	1990	6	50	17	23	4	*Divided*
	1999	9	51	18	19	4	
Good for one Class	1990	2	7	20	44	26	*Good for all*
	1999	6	16	41	31	6	
Middle-class	1990	3	15	45	26	12	*Working-class*
	1999	14	40	33	11	3	
Left-wing	1990	1	26	47	21	5	*Right-wing*
	1999	1	12	41	36	10	

Table 6.1 contains the responses of members to a set of questions about their general image of the Labour Party. It can be seen from this table that in 1999 Labour was seen by the members as being moderate, efficiently run, united, good for all classes, middle-class and right-wing. Of all these characteristics, members expressed the highest level of agreement with the statement that the party is efficiently run, and this perception strengthened over the decade. They were also quite likely to think that the party was good for all classes, although interestingly enough this perception declined over time; by 1999 the largest group of members were unsure about the class characteristics of their party.

The two characteristics which changed least during this period were perceptions that the party was united and perceptions that it was moderate. Significant majorities felt that it was united and moderate on both occasions. Few thought it was divided and only a handful thought it was extreme, and views about these characteristics did not change over time. The two images which did change significantly over time were perceptions that the party was middle class and perceptions that it was right wing. Under one in five of the members viewed the party as being middle class in 1990, but by 1999 a majority did so. Similarly, roughly a quarter saw the party as being right wing in 1990, whereas by 1999 the figure was just under a half.

Table 6.2 Perceptions that the Labour Party looks after the interests of various groups, 1990 to 1999 (Percentages)

		Very closely	Fairly closely	Not very closely	Not at all closely
Working-class people	1990	32	53	10	1
	1999	9	54	34	3
Unemployed people	1990	37	45	14	3
	1999	11	50	34	4
Big business	1990	5	34	48	13
	1999	32	56	11	1
Trade unions	1990	29	61	9	1
	1999	4	40	50	6
Black people and Asians	1990	16	51	26	7
	1999	12	52	35	2
The very rich	1990	—	—	—	—
	1999	19	40	32	9

What then of members' attitudes to the party as an organization which represents the interests of various groups? As Table 6.2 shows, between 1990 and 1999 there was a sharp drop in the percentage of members who felt that the party looked after the interests of the working class. Similarly, there was a significant decline in the number of members who thought that the party looked after the interests of the unemployed. Perhaps the largest change, though, is the number of members who thought that it looked after the interests of trade unionists. This fell from nine out of ten in 1990 to just over four out of ten in 1999. Thus, in the views of the members, the party has increasingly left behind its trade union roots.

There was also a large increase in the number of members who felt that the party looked after the interests of big business, although little change in the perceptions that the party looked after the interests of ethnic minorities. However, the most surprising figure in Table 6.2 is that about six in every ten party members thought that the party looked very or fairly closely after the interests of 'the very rich'. We have no comparable figures for 1990, but in view of the other changes it would be surprising if this figure had not greatly increased over the decade.

Changes in members' perceptions of the party leader are examined in Table 6.3. Overall, members saw their leader as caring, likeable and strong, and this was true of both Kinnock and Blair. There were some modest differences between the leaders in relation to these characteristics; thus Blair was seen as being stronger than Kinnock and Kinnock was seen as being more caring than Blair, but such differences were not great. However, the same point cannot be made about

Table 6.3 Members' images of the party leader, 1990 to 1999 (percentages)

		Very/fairly	Neither	Very/fairly	
Uncaring	1990	5	8	87	Caring
	1999	16	12	72	
Likeable	1990	86	8	7	Not likeable
	1999	70	10	20	
Strong leader	1990	75	10	14	Not a strong Leader
	1999	90	4	7	
Left-wing	1990	20	48	32	Right-wing
	1999	10	39	51	

perceptions of the leader being right wing. Just under a third of members thought Kinnock was right-wing in 1990, whereas more than half thought this about Blair in 1999.

Another way of capturing members' images of the party and of leaders is with the thermometer scores set out in Table 6.4. Such scores are designed to measure the affective or emotional dimensions of images, rather than cognitive calculations of competence, unity and so on. Feelings towards an organization or an individual can be a powerful influence on behaviour and attitudes. The overall impression of the scores in Table 6.4 is that affective feelings have weakened towards both the party and the leadership over this decade. The average thermometer score for the Labour Party fell by seven percentage points, for the party leader by four percentage points and for Gordon Brown by three percentage points. The scores for three other leading figures, that is David Blunkett, Robin Cook and Harriet Harman, fell by larger amounts. Only John Prescott and Ken Livingstone increased their average thermometer scores over this period.

When asked to score rival parties and rival party leaders, not surprisingly Labour Party members gave very low scores to the Conservative Party and the Conservative leader. Similarly, their feelings towards the Nationalist parties grew colder during this period, particularly in Scotland.

One intriguing finding is the growing warmth towards the Liberal Democrats and the Liberal Democrat leader at the time, Paddy Ashdown. The Liberal Democrats increased their scores by nearly ten percentage points and the leader increased his by twelve percentage points. By 1999 Ashdown had a higher score among Labour Party members than one of the key figures in the creation of New Labour, Peter Mandelson. The growing closeness of the two parties during the decade of joint opposition to the Conservatives culminated in Liberal Democrat participation in a cabinet committee after 1997. These developments were buttressed by the attitudes of the grassroots party members.

Turning from macro-level to micro-level images of the party, Table 6.5 examines members' attitudes to any party meetings that they might have attended during the previous year. One of the advantages of this micro-level approach is that such attitudes come directly from personal experience and are not mediated by other means such as media coverage. In the case of generalized images or attitudes to

Table 6.4 Thermometer scores for parties, leaders and members of Parliament, 1990 to 1999

Mean scores out of 100 where 0 indicates that the respondent feels very cold and unsympathetic and 100 means they feel very warm and sympathetic

	1990	1999
The Labour Party	84	77
The Liberal Democrat Party	30	39
The Conservative Party	8	5
The Scottish National Party	32	23
Plaid Cymru	29	25
The Labour Party Leader	74 (Kinnock)	70 (Blair)
The Liberal Democrat Leader	34 (Ashdown)	46 (Ashdown)
The Conservative Leader	6 (Thatcher)	8 (Hague)
Tony Benn	60	59
Gordon Brown	70	67
David Blunkett	71	62
Robin Cook	69	53
Harriet Harman	67	44
Ken Livingstone	55	60
John Prescott	66	68
Jack Straw	—	57
Dennis Skinner	63	60
Peter Mandelson	—	44

Table 6.5 Members' images of Labour Party meetings, 1990 to 1999*
(percentages)

Members' perceptions of Labour Party meetings, assuming they had attended one in the previous year

		Very	Fairly	Neither	Fairly	Very	
Interesting	1990	22	49	9	14	6	Boring
	1999	17	54	10	15	4	
Efficiently run	1990	27	43	11	13	6	Badly run
	1999	20	47	15	13	5	
Friendly	1990	40	33	12	11	5	Unfriendly
	1999	37	38	12	10	3	
United	1990	21	39	14	15	10	Divided
	1999	13	46	21	17	3	
Hard to	1990	2	9	12	31	46	Easy to
understand	1999	1	5	19	35	40	understand
Old-fashioned	1990	10	19	34	28	10	Modern
	1999	8	21	38	26	7	
Left-wing	1990	6	29	45	14	6	Right-wing
	1999	3	27	56	11	4	

*Note that in 1990 61 per cent of party members had attended at least one meeting in the previous year. In 1999 the figure was 36 per cent.

leaders, members can easily be influenced by the press, but in the case of party meetings they are able to judge for themselves at first hand.

The most striking change in Table 6.5 is the proportion of party members who attended no meetings over the previous year and therefore do not appear in the table. In 1990 about 36 per cent of the members had not attended a meeting in the previous year, but by 1999 the figure had risen to 61 per cent. Clearly during this period there was a massive decline in grassroots' participation in local meetings. Considering that meeting attendance is often taken to be a surrogate measure of activism, this is a dramatic change over time. Its origins are explained in terms of the general incentives theory set out in Chapter 4, and we do not repeat that here. Rather we focus instead on members' perceptions of these trends.

Interestingly enough, there were no significant changes in the attitudes of members who did attend meetings in their perceptions of the experience. In both surveys members found party meetings to be interesting, efficiently run, friendly, united, easy to understand, modern and neither left-nor right-wing. Some small differences emerged over the decade, such as a growing tendency of members to see meetings as neither united nor divided and a similar trend growth in the proportion of people who saw meetings as being neither left-wing or right-wing. But on the whole these differences were relatively small.

This gives us an interesting picture of grassroots' attitudes to the Labour Party, at both the macro-and micro-levels. Changes over the decade brought about changes in members' perceptions of the party and of its leaders, so that class politics had declined, the party was perceived to be more right-wing, and it was thought to be moving away from representing the interests of traditional supporters like the trade union movement. But were these changes of view shared by Labour voters? We examine this issue next.

Voters' images of the Labour Party, 1987 to 1997

We have seen some interesting changes and also continuities in the attitudes of members towards their party organization and its leaders over the course of the 1990s. A limited number of comparisons can be made with Labour voters using data from the British Election Study

Table 6.6 Labour voters' images of the Labour Party, 1987–1997

Percentages who think the party is:

	Extreme	*Neither*	*Moderate*
1987	23	6	71
1997	14	7	79

	Capable of being strong government	*Neither*	*Not capable of being a strong government*
1987	75	2	23
1997	97	2	1

	Good for one class	*Neither*	*Good for all classes*
1987	31	4	65
1997	9	4	87

Source: British Election Study Surveys, 1987 and 1997.

surveys of 1987 and 1997. Unfortunately, there was only very limited continuity in the questions asked in the election study about generalized images of the Labour Party over this period, and no continuity at all in questions about the Labour leader. However, there was a good battery of questions, equivalent to those in Table 6.2, which asked respondents about their perceptions that the party represented different groups in society.

In Table 6.6 we examine the indicators of the general image of the party which were carried in both 1987 and 1997 surveys. It can be seen from this table that there was a modest increase in the proportion of Labour voters who perceived the party to be moderate over this period. Rather larger increases took place in perceptions that the party was capable of being a strong government and also that it was good for all classes. These changes in voters' attitudes are the visible consequences of the New Labour strategy of capturing the centre-ground of politics and trying to appeal to a broad group of voters across the country.

Table 6.7 provides information on Labour voters' perceptions that the party looks after various groups in society. In this case there are

Table 6.7 Labour voters' perceptions that the party looks after the interests of various groups, 1987 to 1997 (percentages)

		Very closely	Fairly closely	Not very closely	Not at all closely
Working-class people	1987	58	39	3	0
	1997	42	55	2	1
Middle-class people	1987	13	70	16	11
	1997	15	78	7	0
Unemployed people	1987	59	35	4	1
	1997	34	56	9	1
Big business	1987	12	46	35	7
	1997	17	60	21	2
Trade unions	1987	52	43	4	0
	1997	20	67	12	1
Black people and Asians	1987	23	57	15	2
	1997	12	71	15	1
The very rich	1987	—	—	—	—
	1997	10	37	40	14

Source: British Election Study Surveys, 1987 and 1997.

some interesting changes in perceptions over time. There was a significant decline in the perception that the party represents the interests of the working class, although, interestingly enough, there was no significant complementary increase in perceptions that it represents the interests of the middle class. However, there were sharp declines in perceptions that the party represents the interests of trade unions and of the unemployed, but only a relatively modest increase in perceptions that it represented big business. Finally, voters are less likely to think that the party represents the interests of the very rich than are party members.

Clearly the evidence on changing perceptions of Labour voters parallels the evidence on the perceptions of party members in many respects. The key features of New Labour which emphasize classless politics, cooperation with business, distancing the party from the trade unions and a retreat from high taxation are reflected in the attitudes of both the party members and the voters. Both of these groups have picked up the changes which have taken place in the policy orientations of Labour during this period.

In Chapter 3 we began to examine the attitudes of the members to the organizational changes associated with the modernization strategy. In the next section we probe this issue more deeply and in particular we examine the characteristics of modernizers, or members who support the modernization strategy compared with traditionalists, the members who do not.

Members' attitudes to the modernization strategy

One interpretation of the modernization strategy is that it was an exercise in 'Downsian' politics. This description is named after the theorist Anthony Downs (1957) who extensively analysed party strategies in the context of an economic model of democracy. He showed that in a two-party system parties which sought to maximize their support needed to capture the voter in the centreground of the ideological spectrum, or the median voter. For Labour this meant shifting away from the radical policies of the 1970s towards the centreground of politics and moving from a preoccupation with class politics to an avoidance of class labels. In this way Labour would capture middle-class voters, many of whom would have considered the party to be too extreme in the past. It is interesting that the perceptions of the party members roughly accord with this story, even if it does not do full justice to the complexities of the modernization process.

There were a number of questions in the surveys of members which can be used as indicators of attitudes to the modernization process. To understand these attitudes we have utilized several broad indicators of opinions about party reforms, which can be combined into an overall 'modernization' scale. A statistical analysis revealed that the five indicators relating to different aspects of the modernization process formed a single underlying dimension,[2] in both the 1990 and 1999 surveys. We discussed three of these in Chapter 3, and in this exercise we complement the earlier indicators with additional measures of members' attitudes to this issue. The five indicators all measure different aspects of members' perceptions of the modernization process, and provide an 'attitudes to modernization' scale. The responses to these items appear in Table 6.8.

The two themes which recur in the indicators of the modernization scale are, firstly, the conflict between principles and pragmatism and, secondly, the role of the party leader in initiating and promoting political change. In 1990 a majority of members believed that 'The Labour Party should adjust policies to capture the middle ground of politics'; and that 'The party should always stand by its principles even if this should lose it an election'. By 1999 members were less willing to agree with 'capturing the middle ground', but had not greatly changed their views on the issue of standing by principles.

As we pointed out earlier, the essence of Labour's modernization strategy was to shift the party towards the centreground and in 1997 this paid off handsomely when the party obtained a landslide election victory. Given that by 1999 the party had already travelled down this road, the evidence suggests that party members were increasingly becoming opposed to further shifts of this kind. Members had become uneasy about the Blair strategy of capturing the votes of middle England, but on the other hand they were not willing to contemplate losing an election by rigidly standing by their principles.

Alongside these developments was a growth in the proportion of members who believed that the 'Labour Party leader is too powerful', and also that 'The party leadership doesn't pay a lot of attention to the views of ordinary party members'. Again, members appeared to

Table 6.8 Members' attitudes to modernization of the Labour Party, 1990 to 1999 (percentages)

		Strongly agree	Agree	Neither	Disagree	Strongly disagree
Labour should adjust its policies to capture the middle ground of politics	1990	19	38	10	22	11
	1999	6	31	18	37	8
A problems with the Labour Party today is that the leader is too powerful	1990	6	9	15	54	17
	1999	14	23	19	36	7
Income and wealth should be redistributed to ordinary working people	1990	46	42	8	4	1
	1999	21	47	19	11	2
The party leadership doesn't pay a lot of attention to ordinary party members	1990	10	29	17	39	5
	1999	14	39	19	27	1
The Labour Party should always stand by its principles even if this should lose an election	1990	25	36	12	21	7
	1999	15	44	17	20	3

be reluctant modernizers, in the sense that they acquiesce in the strategy, but at the same time they felt that they were not being consulted about it and the leader was becoming too powerful in the course of its implementation.

The one policy-orientated indicator in the scale refers to the key issue of redistribution, which has been a touchstone issue in Labour politics from the very early years of the party. Interestingly enough, fewer members wanted redistribution in 1999 than was true in 1990. Thus members appear to be adjusting their attitudes to New Labour policies, which play down the importance of redistribution, while at the same time expressing unease about their own role in the modernization process.

Responses to the five questions were aggregated into an overall scale, and the distribution of attitudes along this scale appear in Figure 6.1. In this scale a typical modernizer would be a member

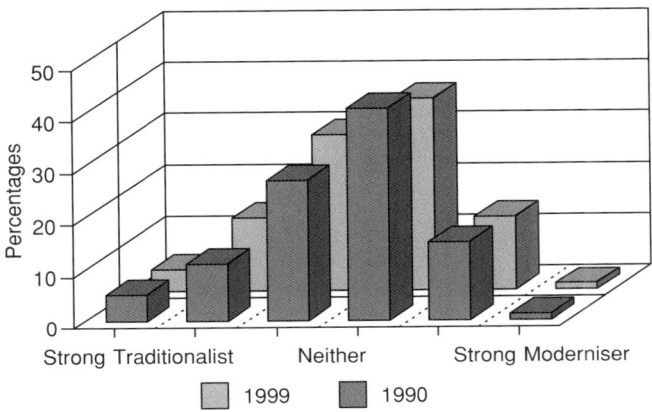

Figure 6.1 The distribution of attitudes to modernization, 1990 to 1999

who agreed with the first statement in Table 6.1 and disagreed with the rest. Thus the modernizer would believe that Labour should capture the centre ground, while at the same time disagreeing that the leader is too powerful or that he doesn't listen to the rank-and-file members. Equally such members would be less concerned about redistribution than their traditionalist counterparts.[3] A typical traditionalist would have the opposite profile of attitudes, in that they would feel that the party should not move to the centre ground, and also that the leader does not pay a lot of attention to the grassroots members. At the same time they would want the party to stand by its principles, and in particular ensure that income and wealth are redistributed to ordinary working people.

Figure 6.1 shows that there are both very strong traditionalists and very strong modernizers to be found in the grassroots party organization, but that most members are in the centre, albeit with a slight bias in the numbers towards the modernization end of the scale. If we compare the distribution of scores in 1990 with those in 1999, they are very similar, except that it is possible to discern a modest shift towards the traditionalism end of the scale during this period. It should be said that this shift is not very large, and is explained by the changes observed in Table 6.8 as fewer members support centre-ground tactics and more are alienated from the leadership. This is true despite the countervailing tendencies apparent in Table 6.8, such as the decline in support for redistribution and a modest decline in the proportion of members who believe that the party should stick by its principles.

Respondents were classified on this scale as 'traditionalists', 'centrists', or 'modernisers'[4] and this version of the scale was used to examine the relationship between the social and political characteristics of members and attitudes to modernization in 1999. Under this classification, some 31 per cent of respondents were traditionalists, 36 per cent centrists and 33 per cent modernizers. The relationship between various social and political characteristics of members and their position on this scale appear in Table 6.9.

Table 6.9 The social and political characteristics of traditionalists and modernizers (percentages)

	Traditionalist	Centrist	Modernizer
Male	32	35	33
Female	31	35	34
Salariat	33	34	33
Routine non-manual	25	32	44
Petty bourgeoisie	22	39	39
Foreman & technician	34	37	30
Working-class	29	43	28
Graduate	38	32	30
Non-graduate	28	37	35
Under 25 years	29	31	40
26 to 45	39	28	33
46 to 65	31	38	31
66 and over	22	39	39
Old Labour	36	34	30
New Labour	23	37	40
Hard left-wing	68	22	10
Soft left-wing	37	40	23
Soft right-wing	12	40	46
Hard right-wing	11	23	66
Very active	38	27	36
Fairly active	27	35	38
Not very active	25	39	36
Not at all active	35	35	30

It can be seen from Table 6.9 that some of the social and political characteristics of members are related to their attitudes to modernization, whereas others are not. Thus gender and occupational status are not closely related to attitudes; males were as likely as females to be modernizers, and middle-class professionals (or members of the salariat) differed very little from working-class members in their attitudes toward modernization. Equally, there was no evidence of a strong relationship between activism and attitudes to modernization, since the very active members were not that different in their attitudes from the inactive.

However, the same point cannot be made about graduates, middle-aged party members or left-wingers, all of whom tended to have more traditionalist views than the others. As regards age, retired party members were rather similar to the under-25s in their attitudes to modernization, whereas the middle-aged members differed significantly from both. Equally the distinction between 'Old' and 'New' Labour members was quite striking. Individuals who joined the party after 1994 are significantly more likely to be modernizers than members who joined earlier. The strongest relationship of all was between attitudes to modernization and ideology, with left-wingers being very much more traditionalist than right-wingers.[5]

To some extent, these patterns repeat earlier findings (see Seyd and Whiteley, 1992: 164) which showed that more highly-educated members were more likely to be traditionalists than less highly-educated members and left-wingers more traditionalist than right-wingers. Overall, though, as in the earlier analysis there is widespread support for the modernization strategy throughout the party and such support is not confined to one particular social group.

The cohort effect associated with the distinction between Old Labour and New Labour members was not measured in the 1992 analysis, but the evidence suggests that the party recruited a new type of member after 1994. Members who joined the party after Blair became leader differed from members who had joined earlier in a number of key respects, and attitudes to modernization is one of these. These recruits are more willing to be led and more trusting of the party leadership than their Old Labour counterparts.

One interesting finding is that gender is not significantly related to attitudes to modernization. One of the aims of the leadership in reforming the party has been to provide greater opportunities for women to reach senior positions. Part of the modernization strategy which achieved considerable success in 1997 was the election of many more women MPs. Despite this, women as a whole do not express more favourable attitudes to modernization than men.

The strong relationship between ideology and attitudes to modernization shows how much the strategy represented a move away from left-wing policies of the 1980s towards a much more centreground position in politics. However, the really important distinction is between the hard left and the rest, with two-thirds of that group in the traditionalist column. In numerical terms the hard left made up about 16 per cent of the sample, whereas the soft left constituted 44 per cent, the soft right 30 per cent and the hard right 11 per cent. Thus outright opposition to the modernization strategy is confined to a relatively small group of party members.

Overall, these results show that there is widespread support for the modernization strategy within the Labour Party. Moreover, this remains true even when the natural tendency of the members to want to stick to principles, and to be suspicious of the leadership is taken into account. Social differences between members appear to have little effect on attitudes, and the one group of party members who strongly oppose the strategy are a relatively small minority of party members.

In the light of this discussion, how do the members view their own role within the party organization? Changes in the decision-making process within the party over the ten-year period have created new mechanisms for policy deliberation. What do the members think of these and what kind of party do they want to see emerge in the future? We examine these questions next.

Members' attitudes to their own role in the party organization

As we pointed out in Chapter 1, during the early 1990s the party embarked on a new strategy for involving the members in policymaking. The *Partnership in Power* report criticized the party's policymaking procedures for being flawed because so few members were able to participate at the annual conference, and the policy resolutions produced were often convoluted or even self-contradictory. The response to this was to set up policy forums with the aim of widening participation and creating a more deliberative framework for developing policy. A national policy forum and eight policy commissions were established in 1997, the former being charged with the task of providing a strategic oversight of policy development. The eight policy commissions covered foreign affairs, crime and justice, democracy and citizenship, economic affairs and social security, education and employment, the environment, transport and regions, health and, finally, industry, culture and agriculture.

By the time of our 1999 survey some 11 per cent of members had attended a policy forum in the previous year, so the goal of involving a wider group of members in the policy-making process than those attending the annual conference had been achieved. But what did these participants think of their experiences? Insight into this question can be obtained from Table 6.10. The results show that the experience of the policy forums was almost entirely positive. By large margins participants found the forums to be interesting, friendly, efficiently run, united and easy to understand. Their only misgivings concerned the extent to which participants perceived them to be influential. About 33 per cent of participants thought that policy forums were influential, whereas 36 per cent thought that they were not.

Given that the experience of the policy forums was fairly positive for most participants this raises the question of what the rest of the members thought about them as a mechanism for developing the future policy agenda. When the forums were first proposed, some

Table 6.10 Attitudes of members who had participated in policy forums to their experiences in 1999* (percentages)

Policy forums were:	Very	Fairly	Neither	Fairly	Very	
Interesting	40	46	6	7	1	Boring
Unfriendly	2	7	18	43	30	Friendly
Efficiently run	26	47	13	7	7	Badly run
United	17	34	33	13	3	Divided
Hard to understand	1	8	12	46	34	Easy to understand
Influential	11	22	32	18	18	Not Influential

*Note that 11 per cent of members had attended a policy forum in the previous year.

members feared that the reduction of the policy-making role of the annual conference would represent a setback for advocates of grass-roots member involvement. To get some idea of opinions on this, we asked the sample as a whole to choose between three methods of forming Labour Party policy and the results of this appear in Table 6.11.

It can be seen in Table 6.11 that a quarter of the members preferred to return to the traditional role of the annual conference as the theoretical source of party policy. However, this was the least popular of the options, and the most preferred option was to build on the regional and national policy forums as the institutional means for forming party policy. Thus support for the policy forums went well beyond the 11 per cent of members who had participated in them during the previous year.

The third option, which had the support of a sizeable minority, was to leave policy formation to the leadership and to have members acting in the role of a jury which votes in support or against rather general propositions. This might be described as the 'plebiscitary' party model, in which the role of the members is not to deliberate, to form the agenda and to choose alternatives, but merely to give assent to proposals that the leadership have already chosen. In practice this model would remove any significant influence which the members might have over the policy-making process. We return to a discussion of this issue in Chapter 7.

It is perhaps unsurprising that there is a very strong relationship between activism and attitudes to the method of policy-making within the party organization. Only 15 per cent of very active members chose the plebiscitary model, compared with 50 per cent of this group who chose policy forums. In contrast, 42 per cent of inactive members chose the plebiscitary model and only 36 per cent of them opted for policy forums. The most active of the party members clearly support policy forums as the preferred option for policy-making.

Table 6.11 Members' preferences for methods of forming Labour Party policies, 1999 (percentages)

Policy formed by the party leadership and endorsed by a postal vote of members	37
Policy formed by annual conference	25
Policy formed at regional and national policy forums	39

The selection of Labour Party candidates remains the most significant power in the hands of grassroots party members. It has been eroded in recent years by interference from the centre, particularly in the immediate run-up to general elections when the National Executive Committee (NEC) has imposed a number of outside candidates on local parties at the last minute. It has also been eroded by the introduction of NEC selection panels for candidates in the European, Scottish and Welsh elections. These exceptions aside, the selection of candidates for the House of Commons remains one of the most important functions of local Labour parties.

In Table 6.12 we examine members' responses to a question about the new system of selection panels for the elections to the Scottish, Welsh and European Assemblies. It is readily apparent from this table that members are opposed to the use of NEC selection panels, and by implication they would not support their extension to recruitment of candidates for Westminster parliamentary elections.

Overall, the evidence in this section suggests that party members value their role in the key functions of policy-making and the recruitment of candidates. In relation to future developments of the party organization, they favour preserving an active role for members in general and are strongly opposed to further moves towards increasing centralization of these functions.

In the final section of this chapter, we examine members' attitudes to the performance of the Labour government. Given that the survey was conducted only two years into the Labour government, this of necessity focuses on short-term performance, and in the long run there will be a need to examine this again after an entire Parliament.

Table 6.12 Members' attitudes to alternative methods of candidate selection in 1999

'The responsibility for the selection and ranking of Labour Party candidates in the new electoral systems for Scotland, Wales and Europe lies with National Executive Committee election panels. Do you think this system should continue, or should responsibilities be give to party members in general?'

	Percentages
Party members in general	60
NEC selection panels	17
Don't know	23

But from our findings we can get some idea of the views of grassroots party members on the performance of the first Labour government to take office in 18 years.

Members' perceptions of the performance of Labour in office

The attitudes of members to the performance of Labour in office were probed by means of several questions in the survey. The most general measures asked about members' approval of the government's overall record and about their satisfaction with the performance of Blair as Prime Minister. These appear in Tables 6.13 and 6.14, where responses are categorized into various social and political groups in the same way as in Table 6.9.

In relation to approval of the government's record, slightly more than twice as many members approved of the performance than disapproved of it. So overall levels of satisfaction with the government at this stage of the Parliament were high. Linking approval to the social background characteristics of members shows that there were no significant differences between men and women or between the white-collar professionals and working-class members in their levels of approval. However, it was apparent that graduates were more critical of the government than non-graduates and younger members more critical than the elderly and the middle-aged. Retired members were noticeably more likely to approve of Labour's record, despite the fact that the government came under fire a year after the survey was conducted for neglecting the needs of pensioners.

There is something of a distinction between Old and New Labour members in the findings, but it is not large. The really striking distinctions in Table 6.13 are between the different ideological groupings in the party. The hard left were disappointed by the government's performance, with only 45 per cent of them approving and 51 per cent disapproving. In contrast, the hard right overwhelmingly approved of the government's record, with those approving outnumbering the disapprovers by more than four to one.

Interestingly enough there is also a clear distinction between activists and inactive members in their levels of approval. However, the relationship is the reverse of what might be expected, since activists approved of the government's record to a much greater extent than

Table 6.13 Approval of the government's record in 1999 (percentages)

'Do you approve or disapprove of the government's record to date?'			
	Approve	Disapprove	Don't know
All respondents	62	29	9
Male	63	28	9
Female	60	30	11
Salariat	63	29	8
Routine non-manual	65	19	15
Petty bourgeoisie	73	23	5
Foreman & technician	53	36	11
Working-class	59	32	9
Graduate	64	27	7
Non-graduate	57	32	11
Under 25 years	53	32	15
26 to 45	57	34	10
46 to 65	61	29	10
66 and over	72	20	8
Old Labour	60	30	10
New Labour	65	26	9
Hard left-wing	45	51	4
Soft left-wing	55	35	10
Soft right-wing	74	15	11
Hard right-wing	79	15	6
Very active	71	20	10
Fairly active	67	24	9
Not very active	67	23	10
Not at all active	54	36	10

the inactive members. In fact the real distinction in the table is between the really inactive members and the rest, with only 54 per cent of this group approving of the government's record. It should be noted that, contrary to many views of the grassroots Labour Party, ideology and activism are not significantly related to each other, so that there are both hard-left and hard-right individuals to be found among the grassroots activists.

Turning to members' level of satisfaction with Blair as Prime Minister, overall levels of satisfaction were higher than levels of approval of the government's record, with 71 per cent recording satisfaction.

Once again, no significant differences existed between men and women or between occupational groups.[6] But, again, there is evidence of a distinction between graduates and non-graduates, between the young, the middle-aged and the elderly and between Old Labour and New Labour. Generally the sharp distinctions between ideological groups evident in Table 6.13 appear again in Table 6.14, as does the distinction between the active and the inactive members.

Looking at Tables 6.13 and 6.14 together, the sharp distinction between the attitudes of the hard left and the rest of the party is

Table 6.14 Satisfaction with Tony Blair as Prime Minister in 1999 (percentages)

'Are you satisfied or dissatisfied with Mr Blair as Prime Minister?'

	Satisfied	Dissatisfied	Don't know
All respondents	71	23	7
Male	73	22	6
Female	68	24	8
Salariat	67	27	6
Routine Non-manual	78	18	5
Petty Bourgeoisie	82	9	9
Foreman & Technician	67	22	11
Working-class	76	19	6
Graduate	74	19	7
Non-graduate	63	31	6
Under 25 years	68	21	12
26 to 45	68	28	4
46 to 65	69	24	7
66 and over	79	15	7
Old Labour	67	26	7
New Labour	76	17	7
Hard left-wing	51	44	4
Soft left-wing	63	29	8
Soft right-wing	85	8	7
Hard right-wing	86	11	4
Very active	75	19	6
Fairly active	76	19	5
Not very active	75	18	7
Not at all active	64	28	8

perhaps no great surprise. To repeat what we argued earlier in Chapter 1, Blair's strategy involved ditching many sacred cows of the past, including Clause IV of the constitution, with the aim of moving the party towards the electoral centreground. It is no surprise that strong left-wingers are upset by this, but since they constitute only a small minority of the overall membership, they are unlikely to have a significant influence on these developments.

On the other hand discontent among inactive Labour members with both Labour's overall performance and with Blair is a puzzle. Why should inactive members be relatively dissatisfied with the government and with Blair's leadership?

Some insight into this question can be obtained from Tables 6.15 and 6.16, which probe into members' concerns about specific issues and their perceptions of the government's handling of those issues. In relation to Table 6.15 health was the most important issue, followed by unemployment. The war in Kosova, which was a transitory issue prominent at the time of the survey, and law and order followed next in order of saliency. None of these issue priorities are surprising.

What is surprising, though, are the levels of policy discontent with the government's performance on these specific issues. As can be seen

Table 6.15 Members' opinions about the most important problem facing the country in 1999

'What would you say is the MOST urgent problem facing the country at the present time?'	
Most important problem	*Percentages*
Health	19
Unemployment	17
The war in Kosova	11
Law and order	11
Europe	9
The environment	5
Cost of living and economic issues	5
Pensions	4
Education	4
Housing	2
Immigration	2
Other	15

Table 6.16 The government's performance on the most important issue in 1999

'and how would you rate the government's performance on this most urgent problem?'

	Percentages
Excellent	5
Good	22
Fair	39
Poor	33
Don't know	1

in Table 6.16 only about a quarter of respondents described the government's performance as excellent or good and respondents in both of these categories combined were easily outnumbered by the individuals who described the performance as poor. While party members claimed to be satisfied with Blair's leadership and the government's performance in general, they were far from satisfied with the government's performance in specific policy areas.

The curious finding that inactive members are less approving of performance than active members in Table 6.13 is explained by the pattern of answers to these specific questions about policy concerns. The inactive members are more discontented about specific policy issues than are the active members. As can be seen in Table 6.17, while 8 per cent of the very active members think that the government's performance on their most salient issue is excellent, this is true of only 5 per cent of the inactive. These differences are most apparent at the other end of the scale, however: 24 per cent of the very active members described the government's performance on their most salient issue as poor, this was true of no less than 39 per cent of the very inactive.

Part of the reason for the discontent among inactive members with the government's performance on issues is that they attached a higher priority to issues in which performance was seen as being poor by members in general. The very active were inclined to choose the economy as the most important issue, and by and large members thought that the government had done a reasonably good job in managing the economy. In contrast the inactive members tended to choose pensions, where most members thought that the government

Table 6.17 Government's performance on a specific issue by levels of activism, 1999 (percentages)

Perceptions of performance on most important issue	Very active	Fairly active	Not very active	Not at all active
Excellent	8	3	6	5
Good	32	24	24	16
Fair	36	45	40	38
Poor	24	28	30	39

had not performed well. Thus differing policy priorities played an important role in explaining these patterns.

Conclusions

Labour Party members are generally supportive of the modernization process which helped to produce the landslide victory of 1997. Apart from a minority of left-wingers, party members were supportive, even though they recognized that it meant a move away from class politics and a growing divorce between the party and its working-class and trade union roots. While there is evidence to suggest that some members had misgivings about these developments, it is nonetheless true that overall they are willing to support the modernization strategy.

However, members are unlikely to support future changes to the party organization which have the effect of further marginalizing them in the policy-making process. It is clear that members want to be actively involved in decision-making and the new structures which the party has created to do this are viewed very positively by most members, particularly the activists.

On the other hand, while many members express a generalized satisfaction with the performance of the government and with Blair's leadership, they nonetheless have a lot of concerns about policy performance. These concerns are stronger than one might expect, given that the government had been in office for only about two years at the time of the survey. One might expect members to give the government the benefit of the doubt after only two years in office, but perhaps these concerns reflect unusually high expectations of the new government. Whatever the reason, the fact remains that of all aspects of members' evaluations of the Labour government and the Labour Party, policy delivery was the area in which members were most critical.

This completes our discussion of members' attitudes to the party and to the Labour government. In the final chapter we bring together the different elements of the analysis and try to examine the future of grassroots Labour Party politics.

7
Conclusions

In the previous chapters of this book we have reviewed the current state of the grassroots membership of the Labour Party and have examined how it developed over the decade of the 1990s. Since our last survey of the membership, the Labour Party has swept to a second, stunning electoral victory. For the first time in the party's history it has won two consecutive general elections with large parliamentary majorities. These two general election victories are the direct consequence of the modernization strategy of the party, first started by Kinnock after the 1983 general election, continued by Smith in 1992 and 1993, and then given a further boost by Blair from 1994 onwards. The political strategy which these leaders argued and fought for within the party paid rich dividends.

However, following the electoral triumph of 2001 concerns have been expressed within the party that the post-election political strategy adopted by Blair and his colleagues is misguided and will be damaging to Labour's future electoral prospects. This concern was most forcefully advocated by the ex-Deputy Leader of the party, Roy Hattersley (2001). He expressed the view that a 'coup d'état' has been carried out by Blair and his colleagues, and that New Labour increasingly does not reflect the views of party members in general.

As early as 1998 Bryan Gould, the former Labour frontbencher, had argued that New Labour was the antithesis of traditional Labour values. He wrote:

> New Labour defined itself by not being Labour. Issues on which the break could be highlighted were actively sought. New Labour

is not Labour renewed. It is Labour rejected, Labour renounced. New Labour is a negative. New Labour is, and is meant to be, Not Labour. (1998)

In this final chapter we do not examine the nature of New Labour, but rather the narrower question of the nature of democratic accountability in the New Labour Party. Our findings do not support the view that there is an unbridgeable gap between the leadership and the rank and file in the Labour Party. On the other hand there are clear tendencies towards oligarchy in the party and a trend which allows the views of grassroots party members to be ignored in policy formation and implementation. We examine these tendencies in this chapter and speculate about the future of the Labour Party in the context of a changing British politics. Part of this discussion will address the issue of whether or not the Labour leadership is taking the party in a new and ultimately damaging direction.

We begin by summarizing our main findings regarding New Labour and its membership, and then we subsequently go on to discuss the future of the party and in particular the role of the grassroots members in that future.

The key findings and their implications

There are several findings which are relevant to our understanding of the future of Labour Party politics in Britain. One important finding is that throughout the 1990s members remained attached to certain basic social democratic principles centring on issues of redistribution, public service and equality. At the same time, however, they had a strong interest in winning elections, given the experience of nearly twenty years of Conservative dominance. This meant that the members were willing to support modernisation in the interests of electoral success.

Members were quite capable of reconciling their principles to an electoralist strategy, providing that this did not violate their basic values and principles, so that the leadership's efforts to modernize the party, first initiated by Kinnock and then continued by Smith and Blair, had the support of the members. We have stressed the distinctive features and beliefs of New Labour, and these originated within a small group of people closely associated with Blair and Brown, but in the lead-up to the 1997 election victory and in Labour's first term, they had the support of the membership.

A second, and related, point is that the party membership were aware of the need to relate their principles to the views of the electorate, but this was not too difficult since in most respects their beliefs are not that far removed from those of Labour voters. As we might expect they often hold opinions more strongly than the larger body of Labour voters, but they were by no means seriously at odds with Labour voters. Perhaps one exception to this generalization concerns private education where members remained critical and retained the belief that it should be abolished, in line with earlier party policy. The view therefore that members are a small group of people holding intense opinions unrepresentative of either the party leadership or the party voters is simply incorrect. They are not extremists, but are part of the contemporary social democratic mainstream opinion in Britain.

Despite this, a third and more disturbing conclusion from our study is that their level of active participation in the party is declining. We define activism in broad terms to cover a range of party activities, including attending meetings, communicating in various forms with the electorate, and standing for offices within the party organization and outside. The evidence is clear that whatever activity one focuses on, participation has been declining over the past ten years. The extent of the commitment of the average member is increasingly merely one of paying a yearly subscription and occasionally donating money to the party when asked to do so.

Such a trend may not appear to be a problem in the immediate aftermath of a second landslide victory. However, when the Labour Party becomes politically unpopular, as inevitably will be the case, it will face the problem that it lacks the political campaigners to argue its case at the grassroots. In this sense the fate of the Conservative Party is an object lesson for Labour. The Conservatives neglected their grassroots party organization in the long years of the Thatcher incumbency (Whiteley, Seyd and Richardson, 1994). This neglect went beyond the point of recovery, so that after the 1997 election defeat they were unable to rebuild the grassroots organization. They undertook the most comprehensive reorganization of the party structure since the nineteenth century and had ambitious goals for recruiting new members. Their failure to achieve this played an important part in explaining why they made little or no electoral progress between 1997 and 2001.

We began this book by charting the changes that have occurred to the Labour Party's organization and structure in the 1990s and it is worth reiterating some of the key points. Compared with the party of 1983 the present party structure is a much more centralized, 'top-down' organization. The various disparate parts – parliamentary and extra-parliamentary, professional and voluntary, central and local – are no longer so free to pursue their own political agendas. Through a combination of authoritarianism and organizational discipline the party leadership has established a more direct line of command downwards to party units which previously had maintained their own distinctive cultures and organization. As a consequence, the Labour Party of 2002 is a more monolithic body than was its 1983 predecessor.

What sort of party is likely to emerge in the future? Can we discern distinctive models of the party organization which are likely to evolve over time? We now more on to consider this issue.

Future models of party organization

The future of the grassroots Labour Party can be examined by thinking about possible alternative models of party organization which might emerge. We can then examine which of these seems to provide the most plausible model for Labour in the future. There are four possible models which cover the range of alternatives open to any party in the future. Briefly, they may be described as the 'extinction', 'leadership-dominated', 'plebiscitary' and 'participatory' models. The first of these, the 'extinction' model, assumes that parties will die out altogether and be replaced by an ill-defined mixture of internet direct democracy, town meetings, citizen juries, focus groups and pressure groups of various kinds. The 'leadership-dominated' model, relies on a charismatic leader like Ross Perot, Silvio Berlusconi or James Goldsmith, who gathers around him a heterogeneous group of supporters, but establishes little in the way of a permanent organization. In the 'plebiscitary' model, the party has an organization and a membership, but the leaders concentrate power in their own hands and the role of the members is to endorse periodically fairly general policy statements and to legitimate whatever the leadership wants to do.

Finally, there is a 'participatory' model in which the party has an organizational structure characterized by genuine grassroots participation which makes the party leaders directly accountable to the membership.

What then is the likely future for Labour in terms of these models? The 'extinction' model can be dismissed fairly easily. There are few social science 'laws' comparable to those in physics or chemistry, but one of them is that no advanced industrial democracy can work without parties. If parties did not exist, they would have to be invented. There are many reasons for this, but the most important is that parties simultaneously aggregate interests and distribute costs in society.

In an insightful analysis Olson (1965) points out that most special interest groups seek benefits for themselves, while aiming to distribute the costs associated with such 'rent-seeking' behaviour among the wider society. Thus the strategy of such interest groups is to concentrate benefits narrowly on their own members and to make everyone else in society pay the costs of this. Consequently such groups tend to be irresponsible about their demands. In contrast, parties which seek to govern are, in Olson's terminology, 'encompassing' organizations. Because they seek to govern society as a whole they have to consider both the costs and benefits of any course of action they undertake.

To develop this point, parties are different from interest groups in that they cannot hope to concentrate benefits on a minority group while distributing the costs among the wider society if they hope to win office, because winning power means obtaining the support of a majority. Thus collective action by successful parties has to be much more socially inclusive than collective action by interest groups. If parties did not exist to perform these functions, then democracy would become paralyzed by a cacophony of special interests.

More direct forms of democracy, such as internet democracy, also face difficulties. Firstly, there is the problem of social exclusion; while internet access is growing, there are large numbers of people in society who are not likely to get access even in the medium term. Clearly, they would be excluded from participation in any system of internet democracy.

A second difficulty relates to the nature of decision-making in any system which lacks structure such as the internet. While democratic debate can flourish in this system, decision-making is much more problematic. There is a technical literature from the social choice field which shows that a system containing many actors with differing policy agendas will produce perverse problems of collective action (Mueller, 1989: 63–5). Such a system is chaotic and unable to produce stable, coherent decisions, unless choice is restricted in various arbitrary ways. Moreover, it is prey to manipulation by agenda-setters, that is by key individuals who control the communication channels. Such a system would quite rapidly cease to be democratic. Clearly, the internet is going to play an increasingly important role in democracy in the future, but its application will not be unproblematic.

The leadership model has emerged in a number of different countries in recent years, and it clearly provides a possible blueprint for the future. In this model a charismatic leader establishes his or her own party with an organization mainly consisting of supporters rather than members or activists. These supporters generally play only a peripheral role in policy-making and are really there only to legitimize the leader and, in some cases, to provide finance, rather than to participate in democratic decision-making. The charismatic leader generally keeps a tight grip on power.

The track record of this type of party organization in winning elections and in governing is not good. In the United States Ross Perot's Reform Party ran a very successful presidential election campaign in 1992, but was unable to capitalize on this success in the 1996 election and is now rather faction-ridden and ineffective. The most successful example of such a party is Silvio Berlusconi's Forza Italia, which was modelled on a football supporters' club. It was in government in Italy in the mid–1990s and achieved power again in 2001, but it performed poorly in its first attempt at government, and it currently faces recurring problems of cohesion because of the weakness of its organizational base.

The best example from Britain is Sir James Goldsmith's Referendum Party which was established with the explicit aim of obtaining a referendum on British membership of the European Monetary Union. Goldsmith took a strong anti-integration position on this issue and believed that the voters would reject membership in a referendum. In the 1997 election the party contested 547 constituencies and claimed to have a fighting fund of £20 million and 200 000 supporters (Butler and Kavanagh, 1997: 149). Its candidates secured an average of 3.1 per cent of the vote in those constituencies, and it tended to do best in areas with large agricultural or elderly populations (Butler and Kavanagh, 1997: 306). The evidence suggests that it undermined the Conservatives to a certain extent, but, as Butler and Kavanagh pointed out: 'Our findings clearly suggest that, contrary to what has widely been claimed, only a handful of the Conservatives' losses of seats can by blamed on the intervention of the Referendum Party' (1997: 308). Sir James Goldsmith died shortly after the general election of 1997 and the party did not survive him.

Overall, it appears that such parties usually fail electorally, and even when they succeed in winning a share of power, as Forza Italia has done, their supporters find out that the actual experience of government is more difficult than they expected. This tends to produce faction-fighting, a loss of objectives and internal wrangling. The absence of a significant permanent organization, a cadre of activists and a coherent set of values to sustain the party through hard times eventually counts against them. This model clearly does not provide a blueprint for the Labour Party in the future.

The plebiscitary model appears to more readily apply to the Labour Party at the present time. Labour's modernization strategy clearly shifted the party in this direction. Plebiscitary politics is really designed to legitimize decisions already taken by the leadership and is not in any meaningful sense a deliberative process involving grassroots party members. In this kind of politics a small group of people around the leadership decide which issues will be put to a vote of the members, and they decide on the framing and the wording of the questions.

This model lacks any mechanisms for grassroots members to frame different questions, or to initiate their own plebiscite on different issues. It does not try to approximate a system of representative democracy in which members are represented in a smaller forum which actually takes the decisions. This model is one in which the members are assigned the role of reacting to initiatives taken by the centre, not one in which they initiate their own proposals. Such a model is undemocratic, but more than that it is inefficient. It is easy for the party leadership to lose touch with its supporters. Initially this occurs within the party organization, but it invariably spreads to supporters in the wider electorate, which threatens the long-term viability of the party as an electoral force. The key problem for 'top-down', power-centred organizations of all types is that power tends to weaken rationality. If a leader can get his or her own way simply by giving orders and tightly controlling the agenda, he or she never needs to argue a rational case.

In this situation decision-making then becomes prey to the whims of the leadership, which is often surrounded by acolytes with no interest in challenging the wisdom of what is being done. There is an old maxim that 'power corrupts', which may be true, but this is actually not the most serious problem. The key problem is that unaccountable power tends to make leaders stupid, out of touch and unwilling to do the hard work of building a rational case for policy initiatives.

This process was clearly apparent in the later stages of the Thatcher government in the 1980s, exemplified by the introduction of the poll tax in the face of opposition from all parts of society. The current serious problems facing the Conservative Party date from that era when the leader became very dominant. Mrs Thatcher's dominant leadership appeared to be an electoral asset for a time, particularly during the Falklands War. But eventually she lost any inhibitions about what she could do and began to embark on ill-judged policies which eventually brought her down.

In contrast to the plebiscitary model, the participatory model is one in which the members hold leaders to account for their actions and fully participate in policy-making and leadership selection through representative institutions. Labour was originally founded outside Parliament and organized around such a participatory model. In theory the annual conference was the sovereign body responsible for making the final decisions on policies (Pelling, 1965). As is well known, the relationship between the Parliamentary leadership and the annual conference was always rather complex and involved a system of power-sharing (Minkin, 1978), so in practice the annual conference was not the sole sovereign body. However, there has always been a strong participatory tradition within the party organization which has emphasized the importance of holding leaders to account and ensuring that members played an important role in the democratic process.

As we noted in Chapter 6, in the 1999 survey members were asked to express their preferences for alternative organizational structures, linking this to the question of who should make policy. We saw in Table 6.11 that more than one-third opted for the 'plebiscitary' model, in which members vote on proposals emerging from the leadership. The favourite option, however, was for policy to be made in the new national and regional policy forums, which is essentially the participatory model. The evidence from this chapter showed that the active members much preferred the participatory to the plebiscitary model. Our conclusion therefore is that although the plebiscitary model appears attractive to the leadership of the party and to some members, it creates real problems for a party seeking to establish a participatory style of decision-making which motivates the activists at the grassroots level.

The key problem facing the Labour Party at the present time is the need for members to reassert the participatory model and to roll back the plebiscitary tendencies in the party organization which have been set in place in the 1990s. The plebiscitary model appears ideal for the leadership, since it enables them to force through unpopular policies. But it comes at a price, and this price is often not immediately apparent to a leadership preoccupied as it is with short-term issues.

The price is clear. If voice is eliminated as an effective strategy for the grassroots party members, not only does the leadership rapidly get out of touch and begin to make mistakes, but it leaves the members with only one strategy if they want to make their concerns felt – the exit strategy (see Hirschman, 1970). Thus suppressing voice encourages exit. Some people might argue, if only in private, that the loss of some members is an acceptable price to pay for a quiescent and manageable party. But there are two very likely consequences of a strategy which seeks to reinforce the plebiscitary model. One is that it will have a severe impact on party finances, since the members are an important source of funding. Secondly, it will weaken constituency election campaigns, since these cannot be effectively organized from party headquarters. The significance of such a weakness, in the face of an ever-more volatile electorate, is likely to grow in importance over time.

In a telling comment on the plebiscitary model, Peter Hain (1999), a Labour politician with a long record of commitment to the grassroots, argues that:

> One-member–one-vote can't replace the feeling of being directly involved in the party in a collective way. It's all right to be

involved in an individualistic way, which is what one-member–one-vote is all about, but being involved in a collective way is what being a member of the party should be all about. It shouldn't feel like being a member of the AA or RAC.[1]

The plebiscitary model will weaken members' powers unless they, rather than just the leadership, possess the right to initiate policy debates, sponsor their own ballots and have an influence on the question wording and the timing of these votes.

Many years ago Duverger (1954) suggested that in a mass democracy a 'contagion from the left' would occur, involving the growth of mass-membership parties which would replace pre-democratic era, cadre parties. However, in Britain today there may be a new 'contagion from the left' occurring in which the plebiscitary model drives out the participatory model. It is characterized by a veneer of democracy disguising centralization and control. The problem is that a party organization bereft of activists cannot fulfil the functions of a political party in the long run. If the party structure hollows out, then the functions of campaigning, recruitment, socialization and fundraising will not be effectively carried out. If this happens such a party will be vulnerable to attack either from rent-seeking interest groups or from more democratic forms of organization, in effect new parties, which have retained the vigour and dynamism created by active participation.

A healthy British democracy requires a healthy party system, and the latter depends on voluntary activity as well as on the votes of millions of citizens. It is true that if a party is undisciplined and divided in public it is unlikely to win elections, as the hapless Conservative Party led by William Hague in the 2001 general election demonstrated so well. But there is another danger of equal importance, that of managing debate so tightly and ignoring active supporters that at the end of the day all that is achieved is the consensus of the graveyard.

The modern Labour Party is increasingly a plebiscitary organization. It is dominated by the leadership, with individual members being encouraged to participate only within a rather restricted framework devised by the leadership. Members are largely excluded from agenda-setting and while they are asked periodically to endorse various proposals, they have little ability to influence the questions asked in these plebiscites. The aim of this type of plebiscite is to allow the leadership to legitimize its own initiatives, rather than to actively involve members in decision-making.

The present legal framework within which British parties operate, in particular the absence of extensive state funding of parties and financial restrictions on the amount that they can spend both nationally and locally in elections, means that the Labour Party will continue to require financial supporters in the future. If the party organization becomes sclerotic and atrophies, there is a danger that the funding from the voluntary arm of the party will no longer be forthcoming. In this case the party will increasingly rely on a few corporate donors, whose support inevitably carries a price. In this situation the party becomes prey to rent-seeking corporations who see political donations as an investment designed to bring them policy concessions.

There are already signs that the plebiscitary model is having the effect of making the party lose touch with both its activists, but more importantly from the leadership's point of view, also with its supporters in the electorate. This sounds like a very bold statement, given that Labour achieved a second landslide in 2001. Since it is of considerable importance to the future of the party, we examine it in detail in the next section.

The decline in Labour's core electoral support in 2001

There are signs from the 2001 general election that the Labour Party is losing touch with its core supporters. The decline in activism charted in the earlier chapters of this book is being accompanied by a decline in the core support for the party. To a significant extent this was masked by the landslide victory, but it can be seen in Table 7.1 which classifies the 413 seats won by Labour in the 2001 general election by the size of the majority of the seat.

On average the Labour vote share fell by 2.6 per cent and the overall turnout fell by 13.2 per cent in the Parliamentary seats captured by Labour in the 2001 election. But there was a clear relationship between the marginality of the seat and the decline in both the Labour vote and in turnout. In the 20 very marginal seats the party actually increased its vote share by 3.6 per cent and the decline in the turnout was below average, at just over 10 per cent. In the 289 safe

Table 7.1 Changes in turnout and the Labour share of the vote in different types of seats captured by Labour in 2001

Marginality of seat in 1997	Change in Labour vote share, 1997–2001	Change in turnout, 1997–2001
Majority under 5%	3.6	−10.4
Majority from 5% to 10%	2.0	−11.8
Majority from 10% to 15%	−1.1	−13.3
Majority from 15% to 20%	−1.5	−13.3
Majority over 20%	−3.9	−13.6
Mean	−2.6	−13.2

Labour seats, however, the party's vote share fell by 3.9 per cent and the decline in turnout was 13.6 per cent.

There were two factors at work which help to explain these patterns. Firstly, as the discussion in Chapter 5 showed, the party members campaign more intensively in marginal seats, and many of the new intake of Labour MPs in 1997 worked very hard to retain their seats. So part of this story can be put down to successful campaigning.

But it is also evident that the party lost significant amounts of support in its working-class base. This conclusion is supported by the evidence in Table 7.2 which is a multiple regression model of the Labour vote in 2001 using data relating to the class characteristics of the constituencies in Great Britain. The model includes the vote share in 1997 as a predictor of the vote share in 2001, together with the percentage employed in each constituency measured by the Registrar General's occupational status coding categories.[2] The specification means that the model estimates the effect of the social class characteristics of constituencies on the change in the Labour vote between 1997 and 2001.

There are two statistically significant effects of class on the vote which are evident in Table 7.2. The first shows that the Labour vote increased in constituencies containing many white-collar workers, that is the Registrar General's Occupational Code IIIN. The second shows that the Labour vote fell in constituencies which contain many unskilled manual workers, code V. The latter, together with the semi-skilled workers and members of an underclass of unemployed people, were the backbone of the Labour vote in the lean

Table 7.2 Predicting the Labour vote share in 2001 from community social characteristics
Dependent variable: percentage Labour vote share in 2001

	Standardized coefficient	t statistics
Percentage Labour vote share in 1997	0.90***	80.8
Proportion of households in SEG 1 white-collar professionals	0.02	0.2
Proportion of households in SEG III(N) skilled non-manual workers	0.24***	4.0
Proportion of households in SEG III(M) skilled manual workers	0.06	1.1
Proportion of households in SEG IV semi-skilled manual workers	0.09	1.0
Proportion of households in SEG V unskilled manual workers	−0.30**	2.2
R-squared	0.95	
F ratio	1911.2***	

(***statistically significant at the 0.01 level; **at the 0.05 level)

years of the 1980s. This was a time when many white-collar workers supported Thatcherism. Now the unskilled working class is clearly deserting Labour, at a time when the party is picking up support from white-collar workers. Although Labour repeated its landslide election victory in 2001, it nonetheless lost support among its core voters.

Table 7.3 illustrates this important point with some examples of individual constituencies. The table contains all 17 constituencies in Britain in which 9 per cent or more of the households were employed in unskilled working-class occupations at the time of the 1991 Census. Again these were households in the Registrar General's Occupational Group V, and these constituencies contain nearly twice as many unskilled workers as the average constituency. The interesting point to note is that Labour's vote share declined between 1997 and 2001 at a greater than average rate in no less than 13 of these 17 constituencies.

Why should the core working class desert Labour in its moment of triumph? One answer is that it is a rational response to the party's

Table 7.3 Changes in the Labour vote share between 1997 and 2001 in seats with a high proportion of unskilled manual workers

Seat name	Change in Labour vote share	Percent unskilled working class*
Blaenau Gwent	−7.4	9.2
Caithness, Sutherland and Easter Ross	−2.5	9.4
Camberwell & Peckham	0.3	10.0
Glasgow Anniesland	−5.3	9.8
Glasgow Baillieston	−4.6	9.5
Glasgow Maryhill	−4.6	11.8
Glasgow Shettleston	−8.5	11.5
Glasgow Springburn	−4.8	12.3
Hackney South & Shoreditch	4.8	9.5
Hull East	−6.7	9.3
Leeds Central	−2.7	9.4
Manchester Central	−2.3	9.7
Merthyr Tydfil & Rhymney	−14.9	10.2
Midlothian	−0.8	9.8
Orkney & Shetland	2.3	9.7
Preston	−3.8	9.2
Western Isles	−10.6	10.1
Mean in all constituencies	−1.97	5.02

*Registrar General's Occupational Group V.

electoral strategy. The strategy has shifted attention away from the interests and concerns of working-class people towards those of the middle class. So it would not be surprising if many of the working class concluded that the party no longer speaks for them. The search for swing voters among the middle class comes with a potential price of losing support among the core voters. In terms of the general incentives theory discussed in Chapter 4, these workers are experiencing a loss of collective incentives to vote for the party.

Does this matter? After all, the essence of the modernization strategy was to embrace the centre ground of politics and win the support of the middle-class voters. As an electoral calculation this makes a lot of sense, since a typical constituency contains nearly 15 per cent of households in skilled non-manual or white-collar jobs, compared with only 5 per cent of households in unskilled manual or blue-collar jobs. In effect the party is giving up support among a shrinking group of voters in order to win support among a growing group.

But there are dangers for the party in this strategy. If a sense of disillusionment and the perception of being abandoned by the party they have traditionally supported spreads to the whole of the working class, including unskilled, semi-skilled and skilled manual workers, they make up around 46 per cent of households. In addition a further 11 per cent of the workforce were unemployed or on government schemes at the time of the 1997 election. Add to those a growing proportion of retired working-class or ex-blue-collar 'grey' voters and altogether these groups make up a majority of the electorate. A strategy of supporting the interests of the prosperous middle class at all costs, might end up losing more support than it gains. What are the implications of these findings for the future of the Labour Party?

Labour's future

The key point arising from this analysis is that the organizational changes made in the party have severely restricted democratic participation and this further adds to the decline of party activism charted in this book. But the problem does not stop there, since a lack of accountability makes the party error-prone and likely to make careless decisions, which can alienate it from those core voters who are already showing signs of defecting. These core voters traditionally supported the Labour Party because it represented them and their interests. If they can no longer rely on this because the party is pursuing a wholly middle-class agenda, they will defect either to other parties or they will drop out of politics altogether and become non-voters.

Putting this another way, capitalist society generates inequality, and if left unchecked this becomes severe inequality. This has been well understood by social theorists for more than a century. Traditionally the losers in this process in the United Kingdom have looked to the Labour Party for protection, with policies such as the redistribution of income, support for the legal right to organize effective trade unions and the provision of high-quality public services free at the point of use. If the party looks very closely after the interests of the winners in the capitalist lottery, and favours low taxes, little or no redistribution, attacks on trade union rights and poorly funded or non-existent public services, then it will rapidly lose its traditional supporters. Quite rationally they will look elsewhere for a party to represent their interests.

This would not matter if the winners outnumbered the losers and unchecked capitalism made everyone prosperous. Unfortunately, history demonstrates that it does not, and in recent years we have observed the emergence of an underclass which began to grow during the Thatcher years, and has not been significantly reduced in size during Labour's first term in office (Toynbee and Walker, 2001). Developments since the 2001 general election do not suggest that the party has learned this lesson and it continues to rely on 'big tent' rhetoric which avoids rather than confronts the hard choices thrown up by the dynamics of capitalist society.

This crisis of electoral strategy may come earlier than expected for Labour, since its failure to deliver on public services was a key factor in explaining the decline in turnout in the 2001 election (Whiteley, Clarke, Sanders and Stewart, 2001). As Figure 7.1 shows, it also had an important effect on the Labour vote in that election.

Figure 7.1 examines the relationship between the perceptions of working-class voters of the Labour government's performance in

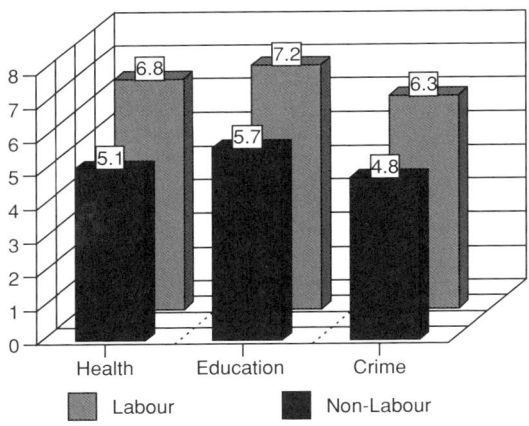

Figure 7.1 Satisfaction with the government's policy performance and voting behaviour for working-class voters in 2001
Note: Each column represents the average score out of ten for the government's performance on that issue given by working class voters who did or did not vote Labour in 2001.
Source: British Election Campaign Study, 2001.

handling health, education and crime during the period 1997 to 2001. The data in Figure 7.1 come from the British Election Campaign Study of 2001.[3] The figure shows that there was a strong relationship between voting Labour and policy satisfaction with these issues for working-class voters. Thus on average Labour voters gave the government a score of 6.8 out of 10 for its performance on health, whereas voters who did not support Labour gave it an average score of 5.1. There were similar gaps between Labour and non-Labour voters in the scores they gave for education and crime, indicating that policy performance had a significant influence on the Labour vote in 2001.

Arguably the future of the Labour government depends upon delivering on the promises to improve the public services, particularly health and education. But there are serious doubts as to whether this will be achieved, and these arise from the post-election strategy of questioning the effectiveness of public service delivery articulated by Tony Blair in a speech in July 2001. He argued very strongly for the privatization of public service provision in health and education on the grounds that: 'private companies can in many cases be more responsive to the immediate needs of demanding consumers. If they don't they go out of business' (Blair, 2001).

This approach to the revitalization of the public sector has its origins in the modernization strategy. Neil Kinnock had to fight battles within the party organization in order to get the modernization strategy moving. Tony Blair built his authority as leader by risking conflicts with the rank and file over such issues as the revision of Clause IV of the party constitution. These were all necessary battles to fight on the road to modernization. But they have been won, and there is a clear danger emerging that the leader might seek confrontation with the labour movement in the belief that this will establish an imagined authority with the electorate.

Rebuilding the public services after years of neglect and underinvestment is a long-term project which is crucial both to the future of the Labour government and for the public sector. If Labour cannot improve services then the electorate, and particularly working-class voters, is likely to punish it for this fact. In this situation the recently acquired middle-class supporters are likely to conclude that no party can improve the public sector, and as a consequence it should be radically downsized, perhaps to the point of providing only a minimal service for the underclass. These supporters would then switch to a Conservative Party which advocates low taxes and a minimal state, and which supports the wholesale privatization of these services.

There can be little doubt that the problems of the public sector arise from years of underfunding, including the first two years of the 1997–2001 Labour government and a record of underspending targets in the subsequent years of that government. Given the scale of the problem it is tempting for the government to seek 'quick fixes' and easy solutions. For example, public/private partnerships have been very much in vogue since the 2001 election and a number of them may work successfully. But the idea that such partnerships will save significant amounts of public funds in the long run is a chimera. The only way to solve the problems of the public sector is to make sustained investment over many years and to work with the management and workforce to improve morale and provide incentives to recruit and retain staff. Privatization is likely to undermine such efforts and in the long run damage services rather than improve them.

Most Labour Party members would agree with this diagnosis and if the mechanisms of accountability such as the policy forums worked properly, the government would be called to account by a party which does not support its strategy. However, the channels of democratic accountability in the party have been significantly weakened and the government can avoid being held to account on this issue.

This development is likely to have two effects; firstly, as mentioned earlier, it will encourage some members to leave the party. But it is also likely to fail. Improved public services are not likely to result from policies of confrontation with the public sector unions and employees, often scapegoating them as a smokescreen for the failure to invest in past decades. If this happens it will not be long before the electoral consequences of that failure will be felt.

Conclusions

What should a democratic Labour Party in the twenty-first century look like? As always an effective party needs clear accountable structures, an authoritative hierarchy which guides the process of policy formation and implementation, and specialists in policy-making and presentation to make an effective case. But it also needs a healthy grassroots party organization of members who feel engaged and have a sense that the leadership is accountable to them for its actions.

If the decline in activity in the grassroots Labour Party is to be reversed the party needs a membership recruitment and retention strategy. The recruitment drive which was implemented after 1994 shows that large numbers of new members can be recruited into the grassroots party by a determined mobilization campaign. As our research has shown, they may not be as active as traditional supporters, but nonetheless they can be persuaded to join and they make a valuable contribution to the life of the party.

A retention strategy is as important as a recruitment strategy. It is of little use recruiting new members, if they find that there is little effective role in the organization for them once they have joined. As the general incentives model suggests, this is partly a matter of providing selective incentives, in the form of congenial social and political activities in which members can participate. But it is also a matter of providing collective incentives – meeting the policy aspirations of the members. Putting this bluntly, a Labour government needs to address the interests of its core supporters.

Now into its second term of government, the Labour Party is at an important crossroads. It has to choose between retaining the essential features of a democratic, participatory party or abandoning them in order to take on more of the qualities of a marketing organization. We are critical of the view expressed by some politicians and political scientists that party membership is unimportant. In our view a healthy party requires a healthy grassroots organization if it is to renew itself and to keep in touch with its supporters in the electorate.

This is particularly true for parties of the Left, since democracy has always been a key component of their appeal. Along with democracy goes the responsibility of curbing the excesses of capitalism and redistributing power and resources to the disadvantaged and the forgotten. An undemocratic party structure is likely to forget this important truth and become a prop to the rich and the powerful, who have no roots in the labour movement and would abandon it as soon as it lost power. Democracy is important within the party because a democratic programme cannot be advanced by an undemocratic party.

Tony Blair is not the first leader of the party to become Prime Minister. If there ever was a golden age for Labour in terms of delivering reforms which brought concrete benefits to millions of ordinary people, it was the Attlee government of 1945 to 1951. It is worth recalling Attlee's judgement about the role of the Labour Party in contemporary history. In his modest, but concise summary of Labour Party principles in the book, *The Labour Party in Perspective*, which was first published in 1937, he wrote:

> Some thirty years ago, when I was a young barrister just down from Oxford, I engaged in various forms of social work in East London. The conditions of the people in that area as I saw them at close quarters led me to study their causes and to reconsider the assumptions of the social class to which I belonged. I became an enthusiastic convert to Socialism ... Circumstances have called me to occupy a position of high responsibility in the movement. Throughout these years I have never wavered in my faith in the cause of Socialism. I have never lost my early enthusiasm. I have never doubted that the Labour party, whatever faults or failings it might have, is the only practical instrument in this country for the attainment of a new order of society. (Quoted in Harris, 1982: 130)

The author of these words went on to preside over the most successful reforming administration in twentieth-century British history. Will the New Labour leader be able to say the same in the years to come?

Appendix

Four different Labour Party members' surveys are used in this book, two separate panel surveys of two waves each. These panel surveys cover the periods 1990 to 1992 and 1997 to 1999. The surveys used a two-stage systematic random sampling procedure to select the samples from party lists of members obtained from Labour Party Headquarters. Thus the sampling frame was the list of party members held by the Labour Party nationally. Further details of the questionnaire used in the first Labour panel can be seen in Seyd and Whiteley, 1992. The revised questionnaire used in the second panel carried many of the questions used in the first, allowing comparability over time

For the 1990 to 1992 Labour panel 480 constituencies were chosen at the first stage, stratified by Labour Party regions, and a systematic random sample of one in thirty party members was selected at the second stage. The same procedure was used for the 1997 to 1999 panel, except that a random sample of 200 constituencies stratified by region was selected at the first stage.

The surveys were conducted by mail, with initial mailings to sensitize respondents about the survey followed by up to four different mailings of questionnaires and reminders, in order to maximize the response rate. The response rate for the first wave of the 1990 to 1992 Labour survey was 62.5 per cent, resulting in 5071 respondents after weighting for non-response. The response rate for the second wave survey conducted in 1992 was 58 per cent, giving 2955 usable questionnaires. The 1997 to 1999 Labour panel survey obtained a response rate of 63 per cent in the first wave, yielding 5761 respondents after weighting. A third of these respondents were selected at random and surveyed in 1999, with a response rate of 69 per cent, producing 1325 usable questionnaires. This procedure was used for the second wave survey purely for cost reasons.

The authors are grateful to the Economic and Social Research Council for support in conducting these surveys. Interpretation of the results is the responsibility of the authors and not of the ESRC.

Notes

Introduction: Party Transformation

1. Until 1979 each constituency party's membership figures were exaggerated by the fact that they had to affiliate to the party (that is, pay fees to central party headquarters) on the basis of a minimum membership of 1000. In 1980 this minimum figure was reduced to 256.

1 The Blair Project: Setting the Context

1. Note, however, that on a left/right scale, Budge (1999: 6) argues that the 1992 manifesto was further to the left than the 1987 manifesto.
2. 'John Smith wanted to heal the party, not reform it. His instinct was for consolidation, not modernisation' (Gould, 1998: 161).
3. Its symbolic rather than practical value is confirmed by the fact that since the Labour government was returned to office in 1997 this particular clause has not featured in intra-party debates about the party's political strategy.
4. One such example would be the well-publicized debate at the party's conference in 2000 on pensions. Whether party members approved or disapproved of the demand from the conference floor for pensions to be linked to average earnings, they would have been made aware of the party's concern with the level of pensions and its commitment to an improvement in pensioners' standards of living.
5. Trade unionist representatives attending the national policy forum meet as a bloc before the proceedings commence to discuss the overall agenda.
6. Further evidence of the trade unions' power is revealed in the sequel to this issue. At the following meeting of the national policy forum in Exeter (July 2000) Alastair Darling, the Secretary of State for Social Security, was asked by trade unionists what enquiry had taken place. His unsatisfactory replies prompted the national policy forum members to demand that the issue of pensions be discussed at the party's national conference in the autumn. At this conference a motion demanding that pensions be linked to average earnings was carried against the recommendations of the party leadership.
7. 35 members of the NPF or 25 per cent of those present at an NPF debate, whichever was the greater number.

2 The Grassroots Members: Who Are They?

1. Larry Whitty, *Report of the Labour Party Conference*, Labour Party, 1988.
2. The private sector–public sector split in 2000 was 82 per cent to 18 per cent. *Economic Trends*, 559, June 2000.

3 The Grassroots: What Do They Believe?

1 In a survey of members conducted in 1994 we asked them to specify which particular industries and sectors of the economy they would prefer to see publicly owned. Clear majorities of members wanted the utilities, water, gas, electricity and telephones to be in public hands but only minorities wanted banking, insurance, the car industry, shipbuilding and engineering to be nationalized.
2 In this context an activist is defined as a party member who works more than five hours for the party in the average month.

4 What Do They Do?

1 This information was not available from the 1990 survey.
2 The median is the middle score in a distribution of numbers. For example, given the numbers 5, 7, 9, 11, 28 the mean is 12, and the median is 9. There are two numbers less than the median and two numbers more than the median, which places it in the middle of the set of scores.
3 We show that a similar decline has occurred in Conservative Party grassroots activism in Whiteley and Seyd (2002).

5 Activism and Campaigning in the New Labour Party

1 As many readers will know, taking numbers means asking voters for their electoral registration numbers as they emerge from the polling station. Once these have been obtained, if earlier canvassing returns show them to be Labour supporters, then they will be crossed off the list of people who need to be reminded to vote.
2 Rossiter et al. (1999: 158) defined marginal as 'the margin between the first and second placed parties in 1992 less than 10 percentage points', and close as the 'margin between the first and second placed parties in 1992 10/19 percentage points'.
3 It is not clear precisely how many seats were on Labour's target lists, because no official list was produced. Curtice and Steed claim that 'the Labour Party targeted 90 (seats)' (Appendix to Butler and Kavanagh, 1997: 312).
4 The correlation between the Labour campaign index (discussed below) and the size of the majority in seats held by the Conservatives with Labour in second place was −0.38, indicating that more campaigning occurred in the more winnable seats.
5 For those with some statistical training this is the OLS regression line.
6 If they were perfectly associated with each other then the correlation coefficient would equal 1.0. If this were true then a 10 per cent increase in campaigning would be associated with a 10 per cent increase in the Labour vote share. On the other hand, if there were no association at all

between these measures then the correlation would be zero, and increases in campaigning would have no impact on the vote at all.
7 The correlation between the Labour vote share and the percentage of the workforce in a constituency who were skilled manual workers was 0.25 in our sample of constituencies.
8 We conducted a representative national sample survey of Liberal Democrat Party members in 1999 consisting of 4442 respondents in the same 200 constituencies used in the New Labour survey. This survey had a response rate of 58.1 per cent and asked the same battery of election-campaign-related questions which appear in Tables 5.1 and 5.2. Accordingly a Liberal Democrat campaign scale was constructed from this survey directly comparable to the Labour campaign scale used in this chapter.
9 Labour captured 418, or 65.2 per cent of the 641 seats in Great Britain in the election (Times Newspapers, 1997: 4). Our simulation model predicts that they would win 64.2 per cent of the seats in the election, so it is quite accurate.

6 What Do the Members Think of the Party and the Government?

1 Dick Crossman provided a good illustration of this rebelliousness. In his diaries he states '... my radical passions have never been based on a moral or egalitarian philosophy. It's been really an expression of my bump of irreverence, based on my conviction that governments and establishments are fools...' (Crossman, 1976: 190).
2 A principal components analysis of the five items produced one significant factor in both 1990 and 1999. The 1999 data had an eigenvalue of 2.13 which explained 43 per cent of the variance in the data. All factor loadings on these variables exceeded 0.50.
3 The distribution of scores along the traditionalist–modernizer scale depends on the responses to these items. For example, a respondent who strongly agreed with item one and strongly disagreed with items 2 to 5, would score 21 points, i.e. $1 + 5 + 5 + 5 + 5$, where strongly agree scores 1 and strongly disagrees scores 5. The respondent would be a strong modernizer.
4 The factor scores from the scale in Figure 6.1 were recoded so that scores from the lowest to -0.5 were coded 'traditionalists', from -0.5 to $+0.5$ 'centrists', and from 0.5 to the highest 'modernizers'.
5 The nine-point left–right ideology scale discussed earlier was recoded into four categories for ease of analysis. Individuals who score 1 and 2 on the scale are labeled as 'hard left', 3 and 4 'soft left', 5 and 6 'soft right' and 7 and 9 'hard right'.
6 The petty bourgeoisie appear to be particularly satisfied with Blair's record, but there are only 22 people in this group and therefore no definite conclusions can be drawn about this apparent finding.

7 Conclusions

1 The Automobile Association and the Royal Automobile Association have members but strongly restrict their participation.
2 This is an official government occupational scale coded from the Socio-Economic Groupings in the 1991 Census. SEG II, which measures the percentage managers and technical personnel, is omitted from the model in order to avoid multicollinearity in the estimates.
3 The British Election Study is funded by the Economic and Social Research Council and codirected by David Sanders and Paul Whiteley of the University of Essex, and Harold Clarke and Marianne Stewart at the University of Texas at Dallas. Working class is defined as occupations in categories D and E of the market research occupational status scale.

Bibliography

Almond, Gabriel and Verba, Sidney, *The Civic Culture*, Princeton, NJ: Princeton University Press, 1963.
Bale, Tim, 'The Death of the Past: Symbolic Politics and the Changing of Clause IV' in David Farrell, David Broughton, David Denver and Justin Fisher (eds), *British Elections and Parties Yearbook 1996*, London: Frank Cass, 1996.
Beecham, Jeremy, 'Lessons from the Forum Process', *Tribune*, 14 July 2000.
Blair, Tony, *Change and National Renewal: Leadership Election Statement*, London: Labour Party, 1994.
Blair, Tony, *The Independent on Sunday*, 28 July 1996.
Blair, Tony, *Speech to New Deal Conference*, Birmingham, 22 June 1999.
Blair, Tony, *Speech on Public Services*, London, 16 July 2001.
Blunkett, David, *On a Clear Day*, London: Michael O'Mara, 1995.
British Election Study, *National Cross-section Survey Dataset*, University of Essex: ESRC Data Archive, 1987.
British Election Study, *National Cross-section Survey Dataset*, University of Essex: ESRC Data Archive, 1997.
Brown, Colin, *Fighting Talk: The Biography of John Prescott*, London: Simon & Schuster, 1997.
Brown, Gordon, *Statement on the Pre-Budget Report*, House of Commons Report, 9 November 1999.
Budge, Ian, 'Party Policy and Ideology: Reversing the 1950s?' in Geoffrey Evans and Pippa Norris (eds), *Critical Elections*, London: Sage, 1999.
Butler, David, *The British General Election of 1951*, London: Macmillan, 1952.
Butler, David and Kavanagh, Dennis, *The British General Election of 1992*, Basingstoke: Macmillan – now Palgrave Macmillan, 1992.
Butler, David and Kavanagh, Dennis, *The British General Election of 1997*, Basingstoke: Macmillan – now Palgrave Macmillan, 1997.
Butler, David and Stokes, Donald, *Political Change in Britain*, London: Macmillan – now Palgrave Macmillan, 1974.
Campbell, Angus, Converse, Philip, Miller, Bill and Stokes, Donald, *Elections and the Political Order*, New York: Wiley, 1960.
Clarke, Harold, Stewart, Marianne and Whiteley, Paul, 'New Models for New Labour: The Political Economy of labour Support, January 1992–April 1997', *American Political Science Review*, 92, 3, 1998.
Cook, Robin, *Speech to Labour Party National Policy Forum*, Durham, 1 July 1999.
Cowley, Philip and Stuart, Mark, 'Parliament', *Parliamentary Affairs*, 54, 2001.
Crewe, Ivor, 'Why Mrs Thatcher Was Returned with a Landslide', *Social Studies Review*, 3, 1, 1987.

Crewe, Ivor, 'The Policy Agenda', *Contemporary Record*, 3, 3, 1990.
Crewe, Ivor, 'Labour Force Changes, Working Class Decline, and the Labour Vote: Social and Electoral Trends in Postwar Britain' in Frances Fox-Piven (ed.), *Labour Parties in Postindustrial Societies*, Cambridge: Polity Press, 1991.
Crewe, Ivor, 'Review', *New Statesman*, 12 December 1997.
Crossman, Richard, *Diaries of A Cabinet Minister*, Volume II, London: Cape, 1976.
Crotty, William, 'Party Effort and its Impact on the Vote', *American Political Science Review*, 65, 1971.
Curtice, John and Steed, Michael, 'The Results Analysed' in David Butler and Dennis Kavanagh, *The British General Election of 1997*, Basingstoke: Macmillan – now Palgrave Macmillan, 1997.
Cutright, Phillips, 'Measuring the Impact of Local Party Activity on the General Election Vote', *Public Opinion Quarterly*, 27, 1963.
Cutright, Phillips and Rossi, Peter, 'Grassroot Politicians and the Vote', *American Sociological Review*, 23, 1958.
Denver, David, 'The Results: How Britain Voted' in Andrew Geddes and Jonathan Tonge (eds), *Labour's Landslide*, Manchester: Manchester University Press, 1997.
Denver, David and Hands, Gordon, 'Marginality and Turnout in General Elections in the 1970s', *British Journal of Political Science*, 15, 1985.
Denver, David and Hands, Gordon, *Modern Constituency Electioneering*, London: Frank Cass, 1997.
Downs, Anthony, *An Economic Theory of Democracy*, New York: Harper and Row, 1957.
Driver, Stephen and Martell, Luke, *New Labour: Politics After Thatcherism*, Cambridge: Polity Press, 1998.
Drucker, Henry, *Doctrine and Ethos in the Labour Party*, London: Allen & Unwin, 1979.
Dunleavy, Patrick and Husbands, Christopher, *British Democracy At The Crossroads*, London: Allen & Unwin, 1985.
Duverger, Maurice, *Political Parties*, London: Methuen, 1954.
Evans, Geoffrey and Norris, Pippa (eds), *Critical Elections*, London: Sage, 1999.
Forrester, Tom, *The Labour Party and the Working Class*, London: Heinemann, 1976.
Frendreis, John, Gibson, James and Vertz, Laura, 'The Electoral Relevance of Local Party Organizations', *American Political Science Review*, 84, 1990.
Galbraith, John K., *The Culture of Contentment*, London: Penguin, 1992.
Gallup, *Political Index*, Report Number 405, London: Gallup Polls, 1994.
Gallup, *Political Index*, Report Number 441, London: Gallup Polls, 1997.
Gibson, James and Smith, Gregg, 'Local Party Organizations and Electoral Outcomes: Linkages Between Parties and Elections', Paper presented at the annual meeting of the American Political Science Association, 1984.
Goldthorpe, John, *Social Mobility and Class Structure in Britain*, Oxford: Clarendon Press, 1980.
Gould, Bryan, 'Review', *New Statesman*, 29 January 1999.

Gould, Philip, *The Unfinished Revolution*, London: Little Brown, 1998.
Green, Donald and Shapiro, Ian, *Pathologies of Rational Choice Theory*, New Haven: Yale University Press, 1994.
Hain, Peter, 'Interview', *New Statesman*, 7 June 1999.
Harman, Harriet and Mattinson, Deborah, *Winning for Women*, London: Fabian Society, 2000.
Harris, Kenneth, *Attlee*, London: Weidenfeld & Nicolson, 1982.
Hattersley, Roy, 'It's No Longer My Party', *The Observer*, 24 June 2001.
Hay, Colin, *The Political Economy of New Labour*, Manchester: Manchester University Press, 1999.
Heath, Anthony, Curtice, John, Evans, Geoffrey, Jowell, Roger, Field, Julia and Witherspoon, Sharon, *Understanding Political Change*, Oxford: Pergamon, 1991.
Heath, Anthony, Jowell, Roger, and Curtice, John (eds), *Labour's Last Chance*, Aldershot: Dartmouth, 1994.
Herrnson, Paul, 'Do Parties Make A Difference? The Role of Party Organization in Congressional Elections', *Journal of Politics*, 46, 1986.
Hindess, Barry, *The Decline of Working Class Politics*, London: MacGibbon and Kee, 1971.
Hirschman, Albert, *Exit, Voice and Loyalty*, Cambridge, MA: Harvard University Press, 1970.
Huckfeldt, Robert and Sprague, John, 'Political Parties and Electoral Mobilization, Political Structure, Social Structure and the Party Canvass', *American Political Science Review*, 86, 1992.
Inglehart, Ronald, *The Silent Revolution: Changing Values and Political Styles Among Western Publics*, Princeton, NJ: Princeton University Press, 1977.
Johnston, Ron, Pattie, Charles, and Johnston, Lucy, 'The Impact of Constituency Spending on the Result of the 1987 British General Election', *Electoral Studies*, 8, 1989.
Johnston, Ron and Pattie, Charles, 'The Impact of Spending on Party Constituency Campaigns at Recent British General Elections', *Party Politics*, 1, 1995.
Kampfner, John, *Robin Cook*, London: Phoenix, 1999.
Katz, Daniel and Eldersveld, Samuel, 'The Impact of Local Party Activity Upon the Electorate', *Public Opinion Quarterly*, 25, 1961.
Kellner, Peter, 'Why the Tories were Trounced' in Pippa Norris and Neil Gavin (eds), *Britain Votes 1997*, Oxford: Oxford University Press, 1997.
Kilfoyle, Peter, *Speech*, House of Commons Debates, 27 March 2000.
King, Anthony, 'Why Labour Won – At Last?' in Anthony King (ed.), *New Labour Triumphs: Britain At The Polls*, New Jersey: Chatham House, 1998.
King, Desmond and Wickham-Jones, Mark, 'Social Capital, British Social Democracy and New Labour', *Democratization*, 6, 4, 1999.
Kramer, Gerald, 'The Effects of Precinct Level Canvassing on Voter Behavior', *Public Opinion Quarterly*, 34, 1970.
Labour Party, *Let Us Work Together: Labour's Way Out of the Crisis*, London: Labour Party, 1974.

Labour Party, *Report of the National Executive Committee 1991–2*, London: Labour Party, 1992.
Labour Party, *Constitution and Standing Orders*, London: Labour Party, 1993.
Labour Party, *Constitution and Standing Orders*, London: Labour Party, 1996.
Labour Party, *New Labour: Because Britain Deserves Better*, London: Labour Party, 1997a.
Labour Party, *Partnership into Power*, London: Labour Party, 1997b.
Labour Party, *Ambitions for Britain*, London: Labour Party, 2001.
Langdon, Julia, *Mo Mowlam*, London: Little, Brown, 2000.
Ludlam, Steve and Smith, Martin (eds), *New Labour in Government*, Basingstoke: Macmillan – now Palgrave Macmillan, 2001.
Lupia, Arthur and McCubbins, Mathew, *The Democratic Dilemma*, Cambridge: Cambridge University Press, 1998.
Maloney, William, 'Contracting Out the Participation Function: Social Capital and Chequebook Participation', in Jan Van Deth, Marco Maraffi, Ken Newton and Paul Whiteley (eds), *Social Capital and European Democracy*, London: Routledge, 1998.
Maloney, William and Jordan, Grant, *The Protest Business*, Manchester: Manchester University Press, 1997.
Mandelson, Peter and Liddle, Roger, *The Blair Revolution*, London: Faber, 1996.
McKibbin, Ross, 'Very Old Labour', *London Review of Books*, 19, 7, 1997.
MacIntyre, Donald, *Mandelson: The Biography*, London: HarperCollins, 1999.
McSmith, Andy, *Faces of Labour*, London: Verso, 1996.
Miller, William, Clarke, Harold, Harrop, Martin, Le Duc, Lawrence and Whiteley, Paul, *How Voters Change: The 1987 British Election Campaign in Perspective*, Oxford: Oxford University Press, 1990.
Minkin, Lewis, *The Labour Party Conference*, London: Allen Lane, 1978.
Mueller, Dennis, *Public Choice II*, Cambridge: Cambridge University Press, 1989.
Muller, Edward and Opp, Karl-Dieter, 'Rational Choice and Rebellious Collective Action', *American Political Science Review*, 80, 1986.
Muller, Edward and Opp, Karl-Dieter, 'Rebellious Political Action Revisited', *American Political Science Review*, 81, 1987.
Nicholas, Herbert, *The British General Election of 1950*, London: Macmillan, 1951.
Norris, Pippa, 'Gender – A Gender-Generation Gap?' in Geoffrey Evans and Pippa Norris (eds), *Critical Elections*, London: Sage, 1999.
Olson, Mancur, *The Logic of Collective Action: Public Goods and the Theory of Groups*, Cambridge, MA: Harvard University Press 1965.
Panebianco, Angelo, *Political Parties: Organization and Power*, Cambridge: Cambridge University Press, 1988.
Panitch, Leo and Leys, Colin, *The End of Parliamentary Socialism*, London: Verso, 1997.
Parry, Geraint, Moyser, George and Day, Neil, *Political Participation and Democracy in Britain*, Cambridge: Cambridge University Press, 1992.
Patterson, Samuel and Calderia, Gregory, 'The Etiology of Partisan Competition', *American Political Science Review*, 78, 1984.

Pattie, Charles, Johnston, Ron and Fieldhouse, Edward, 'Winning the Local Vote: The Effectiveness of Constituency Campaign Spending in Great Britain, 1983–1992', *American Political Science Review*, 89, 1995.

Pelling, Henry, *Origins of the Labour Party*, Oxford: Oxford University Press, 1965.

Pomper, Gerald, Mokley, Maureen, and Forth, R., 'The Conditions of Political Parties: Testing Organization Conditions of Political Party Success', Paper presented to the annual meeting of the American Political Science Association, 1980.

Popkin, Samuel, *The Reasoning Voter: Communication and Persuasion in Presidential Campaigns*, Chicago: University of Chicago Press, 1994.

Rawnsley, Andrew, *Servants of the People*, London: Hamish Hamilton, 2000.

Rentoul, John, *Tony Blair*, London: Little, Brown, 1995.

Robinson, Geoffrey, *The Unconventional Minister*, London: Michael Joseph, 2000.

Rossiter, David, Johnston, Ron, Pattie, Charles, Dorling, Danny, MacAllister, Ian and Tunstall, Helen, 'Changing Biases in the Operation of the UK's Electoral System, 1950–97', *British Journal of Politics and International Relations*, 1, 2, 1999.

Routledge, Paul, *Gordon Brown*, London: Simon & Schuster, 1998.

Routledge, Paul, *Mandy*, London: Simon & Schuster, 1999.

Sawyer, Tom, 'Politics and Management: The Making of New Labour', Inaugural Lecture, Cranfield University, May 2000.

Scarrow, Susan, *Parties and Their Members*, Oxford: Oxford University Press, 1996.

Seldon, Anthony and Ball, Stuart (eds), *Conservative Century*, Oxford: Oxford University Press, 1994.

Seyd, Patrick, 'Labour's Campaign' in Pippa Norris (ed.), *Britain Votes 2001*, Oxford: Oxford University Press, 2001.

Seyd, Patrick and Whiteley, Paul, *Labour's Grass Roots: The Politics of Party Membership*, Oxford: Clarendon Press, 1992.

Seyd, Patrick and Whiteley, Paul, 'Liberal Democrats', paper presented to the annual meeting of the Political Studies Association, 1999.

Shaw, Eric, *The Labour Party since 1945*, Oxford: Blackwell, 1996.

Smith, John, 'Membership is Vital', *Labour Party News*, 4, London: Labour Party, 1993.

Smyth, Gareth, 'The Centre of My Political Life: Tony Blair's Sedgefield' in Mark Perryman (ed.), *The Blair Agenda*, London: Lawrence & Wishart, 1996.

Sopel, Jon, *Tony Blair: The Moderniser*, London: Michael Joseph, 1995.

Taylor, Gerald, *Labour's Renewal? The Policy Review and Beyond*, Basingstoke: Macmillan – now Palgrave, 1997.

Thompson, Noel, *Political Economy and the Labour Party*, London: University College London Press, 1996.

Times Newspapers, *Times Guide to the House of Commons, 1997*, London: Times Newspapers, 1997.

Toynbee, Polly and Walker, David, *Did Things Get Better?*, Harmondsworth: Penguin, 2001.
TSO, *The Funding of Political Parties in the United Kingdom*, London: HMSO, 1998.
Verba, Sidney, Schlozman, Kay and Brady, Henry, *Voice and Equality*, Cambridge, MA: Harvard University Press, 1995.
Whiteley, Paul, 'Rational Choice and Political Participation – Evaluating the Debate', *Political Research Quarterly*, 48, 1995.
Whiteley, Paul, Seyd, Patrick and Richardson, Jeremy, *True Blues: The Politics of Conservative Party Membership*, Oxford: Clarendon Press, 1994.
Whiteley, Paul, Seyd, Patrick, Richardson, Jeremy and Bissell, Paul, 'Thatcherism and the Conservative Party', *Political Studies*, 42, 2, 1994.
Whiteley, Paul and Seyd, Patrick, 'Local Party Campaigning and Electoral Mobilization in Britain', *Journal of Politics*, 56, 1, 1994.
Whiteley, Paul and Seyd, Patrick, 'The Dynamics of Party Activism in Britain – A Spiral of Demobilisation?', *British Journal of Political Science*, 28, 1, 1998a.
Whiteley, Paul and Seyd, Patrick, 'Labour's Grassroots Campaign in 1997' in David Denver, Justin Fisher, Philip Cowley and Charles Pattie (eds), *British Elections and Parties Review, Vol. 8*, London: Frank Cass, 1998b.
Whiteley, Paul and Seyd, Patrick, 'New Labour – New Grassroots Party?', Paper presented to the annual meeting of the Political Studies Association, 1998c.
Whiteley, Paul and Seyd, Patrick, *High Intensity Participation: The Dynamics of Party Activism in Britain*, Michigan: University of Michigan Press, 2002.
Whiteley, Paul, Clarke, Harold, Sanders, David and Stewart, Marianne, 'Turnout', in P. Norris (ed.), *Britain Votes 2001*, Oxford: Oxford University Press, 2001.
Young, Ross, *The Labour Party and The Labour Left*, DPhil thesis, University of Oxford, 2000.

Index

activism 12, 96, 102, **103**, 176
  and campaigning 111–37, 176
  changing incentives for 93, **94–5**, 96, **97–8**, **100–1**, **103–4**, 105–8, **106**
  explaining the decline in 89
activity
  campaigning dimension 82–3, 85
  contact dimension 78–82, **79**
  and donating money 77, 85–9
  representation dimension 83–5
age profile of electorate 126
Almond, Gabriel and Sidney Verba (1963) 92
Ashdown, Paddy 145, **146**
Attlee, Clement, government (1945–51) 186

backbench MPs 17, 26, 29–30
Bale, Tim (1996) 91
Bank of England 14
Beecham, Jeremy (2000) 25
Benn, Tony **146**
Berlusconi, Silvio 170, 172–3
Blair, Tony 7, 10
  Christianity 38–9
  comprehensive schools 18
  education of own children 12
  employment 15
  Labour's working-class and trade union roots 42
  leadership 4, 8–9, 50, 107, 111–12, 144–5, **146**, 163–4, 166
  media 12
  middle England 151
  New Labour 33, 168–9, 186
  News Corporation leadership conference (1995) 40

party modernization 139, 142, 167–8
personal manifesto 8
Prime Minister 26–7, 160–2, 167, 183, 185
project 1–30
reforms (1994–1997) 8–9, 16
satisfaction rating and voting intentions (1997) 26–7, 28
speeches 61, 183
Blunkett, David 12, 145, **146**
Guardian (March 2000) 18
British democracy 176
British Election Study (BES)
  (1987) 115–16, 140, 148–9
  (1997) 36–7, 44, 73, 115–18, 121, 140, 148–9
  (2001) **182**, 183
  campaign survey 28
Brown, Gordon 8, 10, 13–16, 145, **146**
  New Labour 168–9
Budge, Ian (1999) 49
Butler, David
  and Dennis Kavanagh (1997) 112–13, 117, 172–3
  and Donald Stokes (1974) 117
Byers, Stephen 43

Campbell, Angus et al. (1960) 92
canvassing 83, 116
capitalist society 181
Census (1991) 179
childcare allowance 16
civic culture 92
Clarke, Harold, Marianne Stewart and Paul Whiteley (1997) 112
class politics 61, 166
Clause IV 7, 9–10, 12, 59, 163, 183

199

collective incentives and members' activism, relationships between (1997) **94–5**, 96
company taxes 15
conclusions 167–86
Conservative Central Office 115
Conservative government
  defeat of 111–12
  European exchange rate mechanism (ERM) (1992) 7
  general election (1997) 47
  public expenditure programme 7, 10
Conservative Party
  campaigning 130–1, 133
  century 1
  claim about 'old' Labour 33
  constituency associations 113
  European Union 69
  fate of 169–70
  grassroots party organization 169
  led by William Hague 176
  local parties 115
  problems facing 174
  spending 108, 131, **131**, 133
  voters 1, 28
constituencies
  agents 113
  election campaigns 175
  marginal 112–13, 115, 119
  social class characteristics 125
  social and demographic characteristics 127
Cook, Robin 145, **146**
council tenants 126
Countryside Alliance 68
Cowley, Philip and Mark Stuart (2001) 19, 29, **30**
credit-card membership 27
Crewe, Ivor
  (1983) 4
  (1987) 2, 4
  (1990) 5
  (1997) 112–13
Crotty, William (1971) 114

Curtice, John and Michael Steed 113, 115
Cutright, Phillips
  (1963) 114
  and Peter Rossi (1958) 114

decision-making 171–2, 174
defence 54–5
Denver, David
  (1997) 112
  and Gordon Hands
    (1985) 113
    (1997) 114–15, 126, 130
Downs, Anthony (1957) 150
Drucker, Henry (1979) 37, 141
Dunleavy, Patrick and Christopher Husbands (1985) 38
Durham, forum meeting (July 1999) 25
Duverger, Maurice (1954) 31, 176

election campaigns 112–13
  strategy **178–80**
  studies literature 38
  swings 117, 120
employee-shareholding incentive schemes 15
EMS (European Monetary System) 69
ethnic minorities 38, 43, 142
European
  Assembly 159
  Community, British withdrawal 4
  elections 47
  exchange rate mechanism (ERM), withdrawal (September 1992) 7, 111
  Monetary Union, British membership of 172
  Parliament 28
  Union, membership 4–5, 50, 69–73, **70**, 163, **163**
Evans, Geoffrey 36–7
  and Pippa Norris (1998) 115
exit strategy 175

expressive incentives, social norms and activism, relationship between (1997) 102, **103**
extinction model of party organization 171

Falklands War 174
Field, Frank 17
Forza Italia 172–3
Frendreis, Gibson and Laura Vertz (1990) 114
fuel lobby 68

Gaitskell, Hugh 9
Gallup Polls
 (1997) 126
 (May 1994) 7
general elections
 (1983) 6, 167
 (1987) 4–5, 46
 (1992) 6, 32, 111, 113, 134
 (1997) 7, 111–21, 119, 172, 181
  campaigning 82; and Labour vote 124, **125**; members' activities 118, **118–20**, 119–20; modelling the effects on the vote 121–32, **122–3**, **125**, **128–9**, **131–2**
  Conservative government 47
  discussion and conclusions 135–6
  Labour manifesto 10, **11**, 12, 19, 49
  Labour victory and seats won 1, 133–7, **134**, 166, 169
  women: MPs 156; voters 34
 (2001) 28, 47, 111, 167, 176–7, 182, 184
 turnouts 111, 114
general incentives
 evidence for theory 93–105, **94–5**
 model 89–93
 see also selective incentives
Gibson, James and Gregg Smith (1984) 114
Goldsmith, Sir James 170, 172–3

Goldthorpe, John (1980) 37
Gould, Bryan (1999) 136, 167–8
Gould, Philip, 'The Unfinished Revolution' (1998) 8, 12, 32, 61
grassroots members 31–48, 166
 beliefs 49–76
 what they do 77–109
Green, Donald and Ian Shapiro (1994) 90
Guardian 6, 15, 18

Hague, William **146**, 176
Hain, Peter (1999) 175–6
Harman, Harriet 12, 17, 145, **146**
 and Deborah Mattinson (2000) 36
Harris, Kenneth (1982) 186
Hattersley, Roy (2001) 167
Heath, Anthony
 et al. (1991) 116, 126
 Roger Jowell, and John Curtice (1994) 1, 6
Herrnson, Paul (1985) 114
Hindess, Barry (1971) 37
Hirschman, Albert (1970) 175
Hope–Goldthorpe classification 37
Houghton and Washington East (1997) 122, **122–3**, 123–4
House of Commons, election to 91
Huckfeldt, Robert and John Sprague (1992) 114

ideology 91
The Independent 40
industrial conflict (1978–79) 3
Inglehart, Ronald (1977) 65
internet democracy 171

Johnston, Ron
 and Charles Pattie (1995) 113
 and Lucy Johnston (1989) 113

Katz, Daniel and Samuel Eldersveld (1961) 114
Kellner, Peter (1997) 125
Kilfoyle, Peter 30

202 Index

King, Anthony (1998) 112
Kinnock, Neil 4–6, 9, 12, 31–2
  leadership 4, 6, 107, 144–5, **146**
  party modernization 139, 142, 167–8
Kosova, war in 163, **163**
Kramer, Gerald (1970) 114

Labour Party
  campaign index 124, 128, **129**
  change in vote and campaign spending (1992–1997) 127–8, **128–9**, 130, **131–2**
  conferences 20–2, 156, 174
    (1994) 9, 19
    (1997) 20
    (1999) 61
    (2000) 17
  crime, law and order 10, 13, 28, 29, 62–5, **63–4**
  electoral record (1945–1997) 1
  electoral support 1–4
    decline in core (2001) 177–81, **178–80**
    working-class (1964–2001) 1–2, 3, 6
  exitors 37
  future 168–77, 181–4
  individual party membership (1983–1999) 33–4
  internal
    divisions 3
    reform 5, 9
  intra-party conflicts 141
  local campaigning 114
  manifestos 49
    (1983) 4
    (1997) 10, **11**, 12, 19, 49
  market economy 5
  members 38
    activists and voters 73–6
    attitudes: (1997) 73, **74–5**; defence 54–5, **56**, 57; law and order 62–5, **63–4**, 66, **162**, 163; market economy and public ownership 51, **52**;
  own role in party organization 140, 156–60, **157–9**; party strategy 59–62, **60**; post-materialism 65–9, **67**; public ownership 51, 53, **54**, 71; taxation and public expenditure 57, **58**, 59; trade unions 53, **55**
  contacts with individuals outside the party (1999) 81
  demographic characteristics of 'old' and 'new' 40, **41–2**
  demographic profile 34–40, 42
  evaluations of leadership 139, 142
  family connections 39–40
  images of Labour Party (1990–1999) 139–48
  Labour Party meetings 80–1, 82, 147
  level of active participation 169
  loyalty and deference to leaders 141
  most important problem (1999) 163
  'old' and 'new' 40–4
  perceptions
    costs of participation, group efficiency and activism (1997) 99, **100–1**
    effectiveness of campaign activities 83, 85
    performance in office 140, 160–6
  political attitudes 50–9
  representation on outside bodies 85, **86**
  self-placement 71, **72**
  social characteristics 44, **45**
  social profile 46
  thoughts on party and government 139–66
  and voters (1997) 44–8
  membership surveys
    (1990) 38, 59–60, 69, 108, 139, 151, 157

(1999) 24, 151, 158, 160, 167, 174–5
middle-class membership 37–8, 40, 42, 46, 65, 150, 155
modernization 139, 142, 167–8
members' attitudes 150–6
modernization strategy 173, 180
modernizers 6, 8–9, 13, 139–40
opposition to European Community 4–5, **70**
organization
electoral-professional 135–6
future models 170–7
plebiscitary 175–7
reforms 19–26
and structure (1990s) 170
parliamentary 19
candidates 5, 159
performances, elections (1999 and 2000) **27**
recruitment and growth 31–4, 82, 176, 185
role 141–2
of leader 151
share of total vote (1945–2001) 1, **2**
trade unions 37, 42–3, 47, 50
vote share
(1992) 133
(2001) from community social characteristics 178, **179**
voters' images (1987–1997) 148–50
Whips 29
women 36, 68
working-classes 37, 65, 150, 154
and trade union roots 42, 166
years in opposition 59
Labour Party Centennial Report (1999) 31
Labour Party News 32–3
The Labour Party in Perspective 186
Lansbury, George 38
leadership-dominated model of party organization 170, 172

Liberal Democrats 36–8, 121, 145, **146**
campaigning 115, 133
general elections
(1997) 111, 131–2, 133
(2001) 111
Livingstone, Ken 145, **146**
local
campaigns 112–17, 132–3
elections 47, 82
parties 115–16, 122, 128
London Assembly 28
Lupia, Arthur and Mathew McCubins (1998) 78
attitudes, party meetings 80–1, **80**

MacDonald, Ramsay 141
Major, John 6–7, 134
Maloney, William
(1998) 77–8
and Grant Jordan (1997) 77
Mandelson, Peter 5–6, 8, 32, 145, **146**
and Roger Liddle (1996) 8
marginal constituencies 112–13, 115, 119
Meet The Challenge, Make The Change (1989) 5
middle-class voters 36, 150–1, 180
Millbank party headquarters 112, 119–20
Miller, William et al. (1990) 82, 116–17, 126, 135
Minkin, Lewis (1978) 174
Mueller, Dennis (1989) 172
Muller, Edward and Karl-Dieter Opp (1986) 92
Murdoch mass newspapers 12

national campaigns 112–13
National Executive Committee (NEC) 7, 12, 17, 19–21
candidates 159
Committee Reports **33**
Partnership in Power report (1997) 19–22, 156

National Health Service (NHS) 28, 29, 83–4, 93, **182**, 183
National Policy Forum 24–5
Nationalist parties 145, **146**
NEC *see* National Executive Committee
Neill Committee (TSO 1998) 85–6
New Labour government (1997–2001) 13–19
  crime and justice 10, **11**, 19, 182, **182**
  economy 10, **11**, 13–16
  education 18, 163, **163**
  electoral victory (2001) 28, 47, 111, 167, 176–7, 182, 184
  first term in office 85, 182
  ministerial teams 24
  performances
    (1999) **164–5**, 166
    education 28, **29**, **182**, 183
    National Health Service 28, **29**, **182**, 183
  public sector 184
  second term in office 185
  welfare reform 13, 16–17
New Labour Party 167–8
  activism and campaigning 111–37, 176
  creation of 112
  key features 150
  policies
    education 10, **11**, 12
    new policy-making system 20, **21**
    nuclear 5, 47, 57, 65–6, 73
    pensions 16–17, **163**
    regional economic 30
  policy commissions 20–4
  policy forums 20, 23–5, 156–8, 175
  third way 49
  welfare and health 10, **11**, 163, **163**
New Statesman 49
Nicholas, Herbert (1951) 112
Norris, Pippa (1999) 34

Nuffield study, general election (1992) 112–13

OFSTED 18
Old and New Labour, distinction between 160, 162
Olson, Mancur (1965) 90, 171
one-member–one-vote (OMOV) procedures 5

Panebianco, Angelo (1988) 135
Parry, Geraint, George Moyser and Neil Day (1992) 126
participatory model of party organization 171, 174–6
partisanship 92
Partnership in Power NEC report (1997) 19–22, 156
Patterson, Samuel and Gregory Calderia (1984) 114
Pattie, Charles, Ron Johnston and Edward Fieldhouse (1995) 113
Pelling, Henry (1965) 174
Perot, Ross 170
  Reform Party 172
plebiscitary model of party organization 170, 173–7
political
  efficacy and activism, relationship between (1997) 102, **104**
  objectives and commitments 9–10
political parties
  legal framework 177
  participation in 77
  state funding 177
Pomper, Gerald, Maureen Moakley and R. Forth (1980) 114
poor countries, education and aid 73
Popkin, Samuel (1991) 78
Prescott, John 7, 145, **146**
privacy 23–4
private medicine 73
privatizations 53, 184
  'windfall' profits 16

public expenditure as share of GDP (1996–2004) 14, **15**
public services 181
  Labour's performance in handling 28, **29**

Referendum Party 172–3
regional policy forums 175
Registrar General's Occupational Codes 178–9, **180**
Rossiter, David et al. (1999) 120–1

Sawyer, Tom 22–3
Scarrow, Susan (1996) 78
Scotland 30
  Nationalist Party 145, **146**
Scottish Parliament 28, 47, 159
Sedgefield 12–13
Seldon, Anthony and Stuart Ball (1994) 1
selective incentives and members' activism, relationship between (1997) 96, **97–8**
Seyd, Patrick
  (2001) 47
  and Paul Whiteley
    (1992) 46, 49, 77, 89, 105, 113, 135, 155, 187
    (1999) 36, 38
Shadow Communications Agency 32
Skinner, Dennis **146**
Smith, John 4, 6–8, 12, 32–3, 139, 167–8
Smyth, Gareth (1996) 13
Social Democrat/Liberal Alliance parties 4
socialist 'touchstones' 49–50, 53–4
socialization and fund-raising 82, 176
South East of England 30
special interest groups 171
statutory minimum wage 16
Straw, Jack 19, 62, **146**
surveys 51, 187
see also Labour Party, membership surveys

targeted campaigning 115
Thatcher, Margaret 6, 53, **146**, 174
Thatcherism 179
Times Newspapers (1997) 114
Toynbee, Polly and David Walker (2001) 182
trade unions 2–3, 5, 25, 37, 53–4, **55**
  value system of unity and solidarity 141
traditionalists and modernizers 154–5, **154**
Tribune 40
Trotskyist infiltrators 5

unemployed people 126, 150, **163**
UNISON 42
United States
  Federal elections 114
  politics 78
university graduates 38, 46, 155
University for Industry (UfI) 15

Verba, Sidney, Kay Schlozman and Henry Brady (1995) 93

Wales 30
Welfare Reform Bill (1999) 16–17
welfare to work programme 15
Welsh Assembly 28, 47, 159
Westminster, absence of intra-party conflict 29
white-collar workers 179
Whiteley, Paul
  (1995) 92
  Harold Clarke, David Sanders and Marianne Stewart (2001) 182
  Patrick Seyd
    (1994) 32, 113, 135
    (1998) 89, 116, 120
    (2000) 89
  and Jeremy Richardson: (1994) 36, 77, 89, 113, 136, 169; and Paul Bissell (1994) 89

Wilson, Harold 2
women
  MPs 156
  voters 34, 44, 47
working-class voters 125–6, 141, 180

workplace 105
young people 36, 38, 40, 42, 44
Young, Ross (2000) 71